3 PLAYS ABOUT FAMILY

Family Values
The Old Beatnik
Family Climate

Charles Deemer

Round Bend Press

Portland, Oregon

All rights reserved. No part of this book may be reproduced in any form or by any means electronic or mechanical, including photocopying, recording or by any information and retrieval systems, without written permission of the publisher or author except where permitted by law.

© Copyright 2016 Charles Deemer

Round Bend Press
1115 SW 11th Ave.
Portland, OR 97205

Printed in the USA
ISBN 978-0-9965266-1-6

roundbendpress@yahoo.com

roundbendpressbooks.blogspot.com

To My Wife, Harriet

CONTENTS

Family Values: 7

The Old Beatnik: 118

Family Climate: 153

About the plays: 243

FAMILY VALUES

THE CAST:

George, *patriarch of the Wellington clan, retired*
Martha, *his wife*
Thomas, *their oldest son, an accountant, 30s*
Vincent, *Thomas' lifemate, an architect, 30s-40s*
Emily, *their daughter, college professor, 30s*
June, *Thomas' ex-wife, budding jazz singer, 30s*

SETTING:

The Wellington condo in San Francisco. Living room. Stairs lead to bedroom. Upstage exits to kitchen and den. Front door.

TIME:

July 4, 1976. *Act II, scene ii*: one year later, July 4, 1977.

ACT I

Scene 1

AT RISE: The living room of a luxurious condominium in San Francisco. Stairs lead to bedrooms. Hallway leads to kitchen, den, bathroom. Front door. It is morning, July 4, 1976.

VINCENT, 30s, is in the room, dressed in 18th century costume, suggesting Benjamin Franklin. EMILY, 30s, is on the divan, a body under a blanket. Vincent is reading a typed script, "going over lines," preparing for a one-man show he is doing tonight. Finally he puts down the script, stands up and begins "a dry run."

In the beginning, his tone is casual, matter-of-fact; he is doing this primarily for lines.

    VINCENT:
"When in the course of human events, it becomes necessary for a people to change the institutions which have nurtured them since birth, and to assume among the powers of the earth, the redefinition of such institutions to which the Laws of Nature entitle them, a decent respect to the opinions of humankind requires that they should declare the causes which impel them to such changes."

Emily coughs, gets up and obliviously wanders out of the room, on her way to the bathroom. Vincent watches her, amused, but says nothing until she is gone. Then he turns to the audience.

    VINCENT:
(to audience) Emily, the brightest Wellington of them all. Tenured professor of history at Columbia University. Younger sister of Thomas, who is my ... my what? I refuse to say "significant other." Significant other what? My lover. My partner

in life. It is not like Emily to come home to a family reunion. Apparently the last time, years before Thomas and I got together, she and her father really got into it. You'll get the details later.

He looks at the spot where Emily exited, then turns back to the audience. Now he'll play his show directly to the audience at performance level.

VINCENT:
(to audience) "We hold these truths to be self-evident, that all children are created equal, that they are endowed by their Creator with certain unalienable rights, that among these are Life, Shelter, Security, Education, and Nurturing. That to secure these rights, Families are instituted among men and women, deriving their definition and social acceptance from the consent of the people. That when any definition of Family becomes destructive of these ends, it is the Right of the people to abolish or redefine it, and to institute a new kind of Family, laying its foundation on such principles and organizing its authority in such form, as to them seem most likely to effect the Safety and Welfare of the children."

Emily returns.

EMILY:
Vincent, why are you dressed like that?

VINCENT:
Emily! And good morning to you, too! Are we feeling a bit woozy this morning?

EMILY:
Please don't tell me there's a costume party.

VINCENT:
"There's a costume party." Close, but no cigarillo. (Modeling his costume) Who do you think I am?

EMILY:
I haven't a clue.

VINCENT:
You don't recognize gentle Ben, the scatological connoisseur of the Revolution?

EMILY:
Of course. What do you mean, "close" to a costume party?

VINCENT:
We, my dear, are riding a float in the parade. And later I'm doing a one-man show. You won't believe how I've rewritten the Declaration of Independence! Want to hear it?

EMILY:
It's too early to concentrate. I couldn't find any coffee.

VINCENT:
The coffee pot is in the den, not the kitchen. Be right back.

EMILY:
You're a dear heart.

VINCENT:
Dear heart! Is that what you academics say to one another now? Gag me!

He leaves. Emily speaks to the audience.

EMILY:
Just before every holiday I get the same phone call: "When are we going to see you?," Mom asks. I try to explain how busy I am, but my parents understand little about the demands of an academic life. This year Thomas was the first to call, reminding me that it was the Bicentennial. Hence a bigger family ta-do than

usual. So I decided on a compromise. My plan was to make an appearance, spend the holiday in San Francisco, and then visit my girlfriend Sharon in Santa Barbara for a few days. Then I'd return to New York and get back to work on my biography of Mercy Otis Warren. I'll tell you more about her later.

Vincent quickly returns with a mug of coffee.

> VINCENT:
> Bottom of the pot. Hope you run on 40-weight.

> EMILY:
> Thanks. Where is everybody?

> VINCENT:
> At the Gala Bicentennial Breakfast.

> EMILY:
> You weren't invited?

> VINCENT:
> I told them I had to rehearse for my show tonight. You know how your father and I are.

> EMILY:
> I'm amazed he let you in the house.

> VINCENT:
> A grand gesture for the Patriotism of the occasion! Something like that.

> EMILY:
> So we're all staying here?

> VINCENT:
> Absolutely. The family that sleeps together and all that. well, not literally. They gave Thomas and I separate bedrooms, which

is why you're on the couch. I thought of sneaking across the hallway for a visit last night, but I was afraid I'd activate your father's trip wire.

EMILY:
Thomas was supposed to get me a hotel room.

VINCENT:
A little late now. The Bicentennial is the biggest thing to hit town since the Pope. (Quick aside to audience) Did the Pope ever come to San Francisco?

EMILY:
I can't wait til it's over.

VINCENT:
You don't like parades and costume parties?

EMILY:
I don't like history according to Disney.

VINCENT:
I'm glad you made the effort to come. This may be the last time everybody's together. Your father doesn't look well.

EMILY
(changing the subject): So you and Thomas must be doing great.

VINCENT:
Splendidly. You didn't hear, I take it?

EMILY:
Hear what?

VINCENT:
We're getting Billy.

EMILY:
Are you serious?

VINCENT:
Very soon now. I'm going to be a mother!

He moves quickly to speak to the audience.

VINCENT:
A little background. Thomas married June when they were still in college. He told me he already was attracted to men but felt guilty and sinful about it. How could he not, given a father like he had? Marriage was supposed to be his moral salvation. Of course, it wasn't. Thomas and I met when June was pregnant, and I think we fell in love the very day his son, Billy, was born. At least I did. After that, things got hairy in a real hurry, and pretty ugly, too, as I'm sure you can imagine.

He moves quickly back into the scene.

EMILY:
What about June?

VINCENT:
Are you ready for this? It was her idea.

EMILY:
Impossible. June's homophobic.

VINCENT:
She must have matured to mere fascism.

EMILY:
Why would she want to give up Billy?

VINCENT:
She says she's a lousy parent. Yours truly, on the other hand, will be spectacular at it! I'm so excited.

EMILY:
June's a born-to-breed, traditional, wide-hipped, all-American mother. She must be losing it.

VINCENT:
That, too but Thomas and I are just thrilled. Well, Thomas comes and goes. And we're both so nervous! I haven't been this nervous since high school when I went to my first bathhouse.

EMILY:
You, I can see as a great parent. My brother, I'm not so sure about.

VINCENT:
It's such a responsibility! I've been reading Dr. Spock.

Emily has to smile.

VINCENT:
Don't poke fun if you've never read him. Dr. Spock is a real page-turner. "Will the baby gag on his first solid food?" (To audience) "Will he throw up in front of company?"

Thomas rushes in. He is dressed like Thomas Jefferson, complete with wig.

THOMAS (TO EMILY):
Good, you're up.

VINCENT (TO AUDIENCE):
The love of my life!

THOMAS (QUICKLY GOING ON):
What a goddamn mess breakfast was. We ran into June

in the lobby.

VINCENT:
With Billy?

THOMAS:
She was with some asshole with tattoos wearing a baseball cap. Can you imagine a baseball cap at the Hilton? It was very awkward.

EMILY:
I always thought blue collar was more her type. Vincent told me you're getting Billy.

THOMAS:
It's not supposed to be public knowledge.

VINCENT:
My, now we don't even trust our sister. (To Emily) Seeing June always makes him irrational. It's such a turn on.

THOMAS:
I don't want to deal with the parents about getting Billy yet.

EMILY:
So how are they?

THOMAS:
I don't know. The same. Dad talks, mother talks, nobody listens.

VINCENT:
Tell her about the cruise.

THOMAS:
They're going on a cruise.

VINCENT (TO AUDIENCE):
Scheduled to leave next month.

THOMAS:
I'll believe it when I see it.

EMILY:
Mom's been after him for years.

THOMAS:
What about you? You able to get any sleep?

EMILY:
I expected a hotel room.

THOMAS:
Mom wanted us all to stay here.

EMILY:
I'm just teasing you. Hey, give me a hug. It's great to see you.

They hug.

THOMAS:
Good to see you, too. I'm really glad you came.

EMILY:
I reserve judgment.

VINCENT:
Are your parents still planning on coffee and dessert?

THOMAS:
Worse. They invited June.

VINCENT:
Forewarned is forearmed. I'll flirt with her tattooed hunk.

That ought to piss her off. (To audience) June and I go way back.

THOMAS:
I think she has to give him a ride somewhere, then come here. I can't believe they invited her.

EMILY:
Of course, they would. Dad adores her, and Mom believes the world is a lovely place where everyone adores everybody.

THOMAS:
I couldn't stop them, Vincent.

VINCENT:
Don't worry about it. Where's my son?, is what I want to know.

THOMAS:
With a sitter.

VINCENT:
You don't leave a two-year old boy with a sitter on the Fourth of July. Do you? I don't remember reading anything about that in Dr. Spock.

THOMAS:
He's reading Dr. Spock.

EMILY:
He told me.

VINCENT:
She's so irresponsible. The sooner we get Billy, the better for everybody.

EMILY:
I can't believe June isn't a Model Mother.

THOMAS:
She's got some heavy problems.

EMILY:
I knew that. But when did mental imbalance ever discourage a parent? Of course, I only know about my own family.

THOMAS:
Who is due here any minute for coffee. Do you plan to be here? Or are you saving actually talking to them for later?

EMILY:
I don't think I'm up for it yet. Maybe I'll go for a walk.

VINCENT:
And you're the one who wanted to be "a falimy" when you grew up. (To audience) One of the family stories.

EMILY:
You saw the home movies?

VINCENT:
More than once.

EMILY:
Dad really does hate you.

VINCENT:
He didn't show them to me. Thomas borrowed the projector.

THOMAS:
At your insistence.

VINCENT:
I think family history is important.

EMILY:
Don't get me started, Vincent.

THOMAS (CHANGING THE SUBJECT):
We've got to get you a costume. You are coming to the parade, right? They'd expect you to be on the float.

EMILY:
I wasn't told about a parade. Or a costume party. Or whatever else is planned. I was told to be here and that all the arrangements were made. You didn't tell me everybody would be staying here together either.

THOMAS:
Vincent, can you manage the costume?

EMILY:
I'm not up for this, Thomas.

THOMAS:
Dad's counting on having all of us on the float. You don't have to do anything but stand there in your costume.

VINCENT:
Smile and do the windshield wiper routine.

EMILY:
You didn't warn me I was walking into this.

THOMAS:
Listen, if you don't want to be here, you'd better get going.

EMILY:
I'm not ready to belong to this family again!

VINCENT:
Calm down, "dear heart". Meet you back here then?

THOMAS:
Sure.

VINCENT:
Follow the leader.

He turns to the audience before leaving:

VINCENT (TO AUDIENCE):
Enjoy meeting "the falimy!"

Vincent and Emily exit as Thomas moves to speak to the audience.

THOMAS:
My dad and sister refight the sixties every time they get together, which fortunately hasn't been very often. She's so much like him, is the thing. Stubborn as hell. They both devour history, disagree on the meaning of it all, and neither will give an inch. Listening to them makes me glad I'm an accountant: either the books balance or they don't.

GEORGE and MARTHA WELLINGTON enter, dressed as their namesakes, the Washingtons, the Father and Mother of the Country. George wears a wig. Martha is helping George, who looks very tired. When he speaks, we can hear the stress in his voice.

MARTHA:
Thomas! Your father needs to lie down.

THOMAS:
What happened?

GEORGE:
It's nothing.

Martha leads George to the divan, Thomas coming forward to help, and they get George stretched out and comfortable.

> MARTHA:
> He got very dizzy after you left.
>
> GEORGE:
> A little light-headed, is all.
>
> MARTHA:
> Where's Emily?
>
> THOMAS:
> Vincent took her to get a costume.
>
> GEORGE:
> She doesn't even have her costume yet?
>
> MARTHA:
> Now don't you get upset. I'm sure everything is taken care of. (To Thomas) There's some place open?
>
> GEORGE:
> Chinese don't celebrate the Fourth, mother. Chinese tailors will get filthy rich today.
>
> THOMAS:
> I was about to put on coffee. Dad, can I get you anything?
>
> GEORGE:
> Your mother won't let me have a fizz yet.
>
> THOMAS:
> I'll make a fresh pot of coffee.
> *He leaves, moving as if he is eager to get out of there.*

GEORGE:
Don't hover over me like that, mother. I got a little dizzy, is all.

MARTHA:
Where does it hurt?

GEORGE:
Where doesn't it?

MARTHA:
Maybe you shouldn't ride on the float.

GEORGE:
Let me get my second wind.

MARTHA:
Okay, we'll see how you feel later.

GEORGE:
I'd feel better if you stopped hovering over me.

Martha moves away, speaking to the audience.

MARTHA (TO AUDIENCE):
You can't do anything for him. He thinks it's a weakness to ask for help.

Thomas sticks his head in the room.

THOMAS:
Anybody going to want pastries?

GEORGE:
Nothing for me, son.

MARTHA:
I'm so full, I'll probably skip lunch.

Thomas exits.

GEORGE:
He seem okay to you?

MARTHA:
Yes.

GEORGE:
He acts like he's upset about something.

MARTHA:
I don't think he's ever been happier.

GEORGE:
I'm sure Jack the Ripper was happy, too.

MARTHA:
George, don't.

GEORGE:
Happiness doesn't really have much to do with anything, does it? As far as right and wrong are concerned?

MARTHA:
George, please don't start a row, today of all days.

GEORGE:
Every time I see June, I think of Billy having no father in the house.

MARTHA:
As many children grow up today with one parent as two. Billy will be fine.

GEORGE:
Kids need both parents. The downfall of the family is going to be the downfall of the country, mark my word. I'm glad I won't be around to see it.

MARTHA:
What has made you so morbid today?

GEORGE:
You ever wonder if we live up to our roots? I mean, look at us. What would our Founding Fathers think if they were alive today? I shudder to imagine.

MARTHA:
When you feel bad, it touches everything you think about.

GEORGE:
You don't believe the world's going to hell in a hand-basket?

MARTHA:
I think when you get your second wind, you won't be talking like that. (Changing the subject) What a surprise running into June. How did she look to you?

GEORGE:
Tired.

MARTHA:
I thought she looked ill. I bet she's not eating right. (To audience) Thomas always did most of the cooking.

GEORGE:
I think she's just tired, mother. Of course she'd be tired, raising a son by herself. I worry about her and Billy all alone in that big house.

MARTHA:
I'm sure they do fine.

GEORGE:
You don't worry about her?

MARTHA:
Not really. You know who I worry about.

GEORGE:
And you know what I have to say about it.

MARTHA:
Emily's as much a part of my flesh as Thomas is. I can't dismiss her.

Thomas enters with coffee.

THOMAS:
Here we are.

MARTHA:
I was just telling George that June didn't look well. Didn't you think so?

THOMAS:
How so?

GEORGE:
Very tired.

THOMAS:
She left Billy with a sitter, Dad. Not too much fatigue in that.

MARTHA:
She always did drive herself too hard.

GEORGE:
And now she has no help.

THOMAS (IGNORING THIS):
She still blames herself for not finishing school. She blames herself for not being more than a housewife. She even blames herself, you know, for how we turned out.

MARTHA:
She once told me she always wanted to be a singer. A vocalist, she called it. She used to stop by a piano bar and sing along when she was single, always brought down the house. The pianist told her she reminded him of young Peggy Lee. Imagine telling that to an impressionable young woman.

THOMAS:
She does have a good voice, actually. But I can't picture her with the gumption to pay the dues it would take.

MARTHA:
Well, she has Billy to think about now.

GEORGE:
Not easy being a single parent. Not easy at all.

THOMAS:
Will you excuse me a minute?

He moves away and speaks to the audience.

THOMAS:
I felt like I was suffocating. Obviously I was the Fallen Son in Dad's eyes, but I'd learned to let his little digs go in one ear and out the other. Now, what with the stress of Emily being here, and everybody wondering when she and Dad would get into it; and June on her way over, which I considered the worst timing because Dad was bound to bring up Billy. I needed a couple of

deep breaths and a battery charge, like immediately.

Thomas quickly exits.

MARTHA:
Why must you torment him? He doesn't want to talk about June.

GEORGE:
I'm not forcing him to talk about her.

MARTHA:
You keep bringing her up.

GEORGE:
You brought her up!

MARTHA:
I think he still cares for her.

GEORGE:
Mother, he's a homosexual. It isn't a passing phase he's in.

MARTHA:
I'm perfectly aware of that.

GEORGE:
So he doesn't still hold a torch for June. Never did. She's not his element, so to speak.

MARTHA:
He can still care for her, and I think he does. This is all much harder on him than he admits. Or than you admit.

GEORGE:
I doubt that very seriously.

MARTHA:
Why can't you give him the benefit of the doubt?

GEORGE:
Why should I? They kept me awake all night.

MARTHA:
Who?

GEORGE:
The two of them. I kept expecting to hear someone sneak across the hall.

MARTHA:
What a thing to lose sleep over!

GEORGE:
I wouldn't put it past them.

MARTHA:
Serves you right, making them use separate bedrooms. Long as they've been living together now.

GEORGE:
I'm not running a cat house.

MARTHA:
You're just itching for a fight with Vincent, aren't you?

GEORGE:
I can be polite to him. It doesn't mean I approve of him or encourage what they do.

MARTHA:
You've never appreciated how difficult it was for Thomas to come out.

GEORGE:
Since when is lust difficult? It's doing the right thing that's hard.

MARTHA:
That's not fair. He loves Vincent.

GEORGE:
We'll never agree, mother.

MARTHA:
You don't want to talk about Emily, well, I don't want to talk about this. I would like this to be a special day. We may not have everybody together again.

The doorbell rings. George sits up.

MARTHA:
You don't have to get up.

Thomas rushes in and to the door.

THOMAS:
I'll get it.

Thomas answers the door. JUNE walks in. She's pretty but doesn't take advantage of it and looks, in fact, like she could use some sleep.

THOMAS:
Hello. Come in.

JUNE:
They said it would be all right to come over.

THOMAS:
Of course, it's all right. Coffee?

JUNE:
Yes, thanks. I love your costume.

THOMAS:
Still sugar and cream?

June smiles and nods. Thomas leaves to fetch coffee.

MARTHA:
I'm so glad you could stop by.

GEORGE:
Wish you had Billy.

JUNE:
To be honest, it's nice to have some time to myself.

MARTHA:
We'll have you to dinner soon. Right after we get back from our cruise.

JUNE:
A cruise!

MARTHA:
We leave next month. It only took me thirty years to get him to take me.

GEORGE:
We're not on the high seas yet, mother.

MARTHA:
No backing out on me! Listen to him.

JUNE:
Where are you going?

MARTHA:
The Bahamas. We'll be gone 10 days.

GEORGE:
Probably seasick the whole time.

MARTHA:
He's been in one of his moods all morning.

GEORGE (IGNORING THIS):
So how's the Billy boy doing?

JUNE:
He's great.

GEORGE:
I thought of taking him on the cruise. Of course, I knew you wouldn't give him up for that long.

June moves to speak to e audience:

JUNE (TO AUDIENCE):
So they didn't know yet. I guessed as much since they hadn't said anything about it at the Hilton. It was just like Thomas to put off something important to the last possible moment. Thomas is the great procrastinator.

MARTHA:
What an interesting young man you were with.

JUNE (MOVING BACK INTO SCENE):
Andy? He's in my jazz improv class.

GEORGE:
Your what?

JUNE:
I'm taking some music classes at night.

GEORGE:
I didn't know that.

MARTHA:
Oh, you did so. His memory's going.

JUNE:
I don't think I told either of you.

GEORGE:
That keeps you pretty busy, doesn't it?

JUNE:
Too busy, I'm afraid.

GEORGE:
Keeping care of Billy is a full-time job in itself.

JUNE (WANTING TO GET OUT OF THIS):
It can be, that's for sure. I wonder if Thomas needs any help.

But he is just now entering.

MARTHA:
June is taking a music class!

THOMAS:
Really? You finally bit the bullet.

JUNE:
Yep.

THOMAS:
I didn't ask if you wanted a pastry.

JUNE:
No thanks.

MARTHA:
Does anyone mind if I take my coffee upstairs? I want to freshen up.

THOMAS:
Of course not.

MARTHA:
George? I want to touch up your wig. You probably are ready to get out from under it.

GEORGE:
What she's trying to say is, You two probably want some time alone.

MARTHA:
Now that you mention it, I'm sure they do. George?

Martha and George start upstairs to their bedroom. Martha tries to help him but he pushes her away.

GEORGE:
Quit hovering over me.

George starts upstairs. On her way out behind him, Martha speaks to the audience.

MARTHA (TO AUDIENCE):
I gave up trying to change him long ago. The glass on the table is never full, and whether it's half-empty or half-full is completely up to you.

She exits behind George.

JUNE:
Where's Vincent?

THOMAS:
He's helping Emily get a costume.

JUNE:
So she finally broke down and came home.

THOMAS:
Only in a manner of speaking. I think she's already ready to leave.

JUNE:
She still teaching at Columbia?

THOMAS:
Oh, yes. Tenure and everything.

JUNE:
I'm sorry I missed her.

THOMAS:
June, I don't want Dad to find out what's coming down sooner than he has to. Especially not today. Everybody's looking at this like it's the Last Family Reunion.

JUNE:
I certainly don't plan on telling him.

THOMAS:
I just wanted to touch bases with you. I'll tell Mom first and let her break the news to him.

A pause.

THOMAS:
Not getting cold feet are you?

JUNE:
I don't think so.

THOMAS:
That's not very encouraging.

JUNE:
I'm fine. It's just going to be quite a change.

THOMAS:
You're doing the right thing.

JUNE:
The only part that worries me is Vincent. He and I need to reach an understanding.

THOMAS:
I've wanted you two to be friends from the start.

JUNE:
I'm not sure that can happen. But we can be civil, for Billy's sake. Where do you think Vincent's at with all this?

THOMAS:
You said some pretty vicious things about him.

JUNE:
All of us said things we regret.

THOMAS:
True enough.

JUNE:
Billy will pick up on any animosity between us.

THOMAS:
I'll talk to Vincent and test the waters. Maybe we can sit down together.

JUNE:
Thanks, Thomas.

THOMAS:
What's your schedule?

JUNE:
I'm only in the city for the day, so later would be great if you have time.

THOMAS:
We have a party tonight but there's a break after the parade. You could come by around four, and we could all go out for a drink.

JUNE:
If Vincent's up to it, that would be perfect.

THOMAS:
So you're studying music again.

June moves forward to speak to the audience:

JUNE (TO AUDIENCE):
I hate it when he pretends to be interested in what I'm doing. Especially about something as important to me as music. Money was never a problem with us but would he buy me a piano? I'm a musician, for God's sake, I need a piano as much as he needs a calculator. But he never took, he still doesn't take, my music seriously. It's just my hobby, as far as he's concerned. So when he starts pretending he's interested in what I'm doing, I just turn him off, I might as well be wearing a hearing aid and flipping

the switch.

The door opens and Vincent enters.

> VINCENT:
> Oops, didn't mean to interrupt.

He starts out.

> THOMAS:
> Vincent, wait a minute. We need to talk.

> VINCENT:
> Emily won't come in unless the coast is clear. Where are your parents?

> THOMAS:
> Upstairs.

Vincent calls into the hallway.

> VINCENT:
> The coast is clear! (To the audience) Tenure at Columbia, and she's afraid to face her parents.

He moves into the room, leaving the door open.

> JUNE:
> I like your costume. Ben Franklin, right?

> VINCENT:
> A kind word? What are you setting me up for?

> JUNE:
> I'd better be going.

THOMAS:
Vincent, I was thinking later the three of us could get together for a drink. We need to find a way to all work together, for Billy's sake.

Emily enters. She is dressed in a period costume.

EMILY:
Hi, June.

JUNE:
What a surprise. I hear you got tenure.

EMILY:
A couple years ago, actually.

JUNE:
Congratulations. So, Thomas, I'll call later.

THOMAS:
Great.

JUNE:
Nice seeing you, Emily.

June starts out.

VINCENT:
Farewell to you, too! (To the audience) She can't stand to be in the same room with me.

June moves quickly to speak to the audience.

JUNE:
No, that's not true. I've never hated Vincent the way I think I'd hate "the other woman," if Thomas had left me for one. That's what I was afraid was going to happen. After Billy was

born, nothing was the same between us, and I thought Thomas was having an affair. With a woman, I mean. But when you lose your spouse, the person you love, the person you expect to spend the rest of your life with, the father of your child, when you lose him to another man, I don't know how to describe the feeling. I was shocked. I hadn't seen it coming, not that way, not a clue. It's like waking up on another planet. Well, I flipped out, is what happened.
She exits.

      VINCENT:
What do you think?

      THOMAS:
I'm worried about her.

      VINCENT:
About the costume! We didn't have much of a selection.

      THOMAS:
Looks fine.

      VINCENT:
Now what persona will you use?

      EMILY:
Vincent, for Christ's sake …

      VINCENT:
You have to be someone, "dear heart."

      EMILY:
Fine. I'm Mercy Otis Warren.

      THOMAS:
Who the hell is that?

EMILY:
America's first playwright. Younger sister of James Otis.

THOMAS:
That explains everything. Who's James Otis?

EMILY:
Are you kidding me? Vincent, tell him.

VINCENT:
I'm just a dirty old man, what do I know? I write clever one-liners for Poor Richard's Almanac. (To audience) Benjamin Franklin also had the best collection of scatological literature in the colonies. Definitely our most anal Founding Father.

EMILY:
Otis is the man who first said, "No taxation without representation!"

THOMAS:
I thought that was Patrick Henry.

VINCENT:
That's "Give me puberty or give me death!"

EMILY:
Otis is one of the more fascinating characters in the revolution. He was a conservative, he didn't want a revolution, he wanted American representation in the British Parliament.

VINCENT:
Really? So tell me, who was the first American drag queen? (To audience) This should be interesting.

EMILY:
Not my area of specialization, Vincent.

VINCENT:
If it ain't Mom and Apple Pie, it ain't in the history books. Same old story.

EMILY:
You get no argument from me. History is what the winners tell the losers.

CROSS FADE to upstairs bedroom. George is out of his wig, stretched out on the bed, talking to Martha.

MARTHA:
You worry me. You really don't feel well, do you?

GEORGE:
I haven't felt well in years.

MARTHA:
I mean right now. Promise me you'll see the doctor before we leave on the cruise.

GEORGE:
Pretty short notice.

MARTHA:
We have time. He'll let you in.

GEORGE:
I'm getting old, mother. Doctors can't do a thing about it.

MARTHA:
You're not that old.

GEORGE:
I feel older every day.

MARTHA:
Wait til we get to sea. The salt air will do wonders for you.

GEORGE:
Probably spend the whole trip barfing.

MARTHA:
You're just determined to be miserable today, aren't you? Well, I'm not letting you bring me down to your level. If you want to feel sorry for yourself, be my guest. I'm going to enjoy the family being together again..

GEORGE:
Is that what we are? A family?

MARTHA:
Of course we're a family. What a thing to say.

GEORGE:
Not a family the way it used to be. How many homosexuals were in your parents' family?

MARTHA:
Things were different then.

GEORGE:
You can say that again.

MARTHA:
There probably were more homosexuals than we knew about, George, only they kept to themselves.

GEORGE:
That's exactly what I mean. It was unthinkable to flaunt your sex life in public. A disgrace.

MARTHA:
Thomas is not a disgrace. He can't help the way he is.

GEORGE:
Does that give them license to keep everybody awake all night?

MARTHA:
You kept yourself awake, worrying about them! I'm going downstairs. Please try to relax. You have time for a little nap.

GEORGE:
I'm not sleepy.

MARTHA:
You want to come downstairs with me?

GEORGE:
I'll be down directly, mother.

MARTHA:
You're sure you're up to being on the float?

GEORGE:
I'll be fine. Just give me a minute to get my second wind.

George watches Martha leave. Then he goes to a closet and takes out a blue canvas bag. He stares at it. CROSS FADE to downstairs.

EMILY:
I'm amazed at the change in June's attitude.

THOMAS:
She just hates the responsibility of being a parent. Apparently she's going to try and do something with her music.

Vincent is the first to see Martha coming down the stairs.

VINCENT:
All hail the Mother of Our Country!

He moves to her, taking her arm.

VINCENT:
What can I get you? Coffee? A drink?

MARTHA:
Emily!

EMILY:
Hi, Mom.

They embrace a bit stiffly.

MARTHA:
I'm so happy you were able to come. I know how busy you are.

EMILY:
Well, here I am. (Modeling her costume:) I didn't know exactly what I was getting into.

THOMAS:
She's America's first playwright. What was her name?

EMILY:
Mercy Otis Warren.

MARTHA:
Really? Isn't that marvelous?

EMILY:
You look good, Mom. How's Dad doing?

MARTHA:
I'm worried about him. He had a dizzy spell this morning, and you know how stubborn he can be about seeing a doctor. We're leaving on a cruise next week.

EMILY:
So I hear.

MARTHA:
I want him to get a checkup before we go.

THOMAS:
Is he feeling well enough to do the parade?

MARTHA:
We'll see how he feels after his nap.

VINCENT:
I'm sure we can find a stool for him on the float. At least he won't have to be on his feet.

MARTHA:
How thoughtful.

EMILY:
I'm nervous about seeing him. We got in such a brawl the last time.

THOMAS:
Don't talk about college and the sixties, and you'll be fine.

VINCENT:
Try peaceful coexistence. Look at me. I know he doesn't approve of me, but here I am!

MARTHA:
That's not true, Vincent. Of course he likes you.

THOMAS:
Mother, please.

VINCENT:
I'm a guest in his house, at any rate. There's definite signs of progress there.

MARTHA:
It's not you two so much. He worries more about Billy not having a father in the house.

Thomas and Vincent exchange a knowing glance.

THOMAS:
Billy has a father.

MARTHA:
I know that. George is old-fashioned. He thinks children need two parents in the home.

A pause.

THOMAS:
Mom, there's something I should tell you. (To Vincent) Unless you object.

VINCENT:
Your decision. (To audience) I'm not touching that with a ten-foot you-know-what.

THOMAS (TO VINCENT):
Maybe Mom can break it to him on the cruise.

EMILY:
I think it's a good idea, Thomas.

MARTHA:
What are you talking about?

THOMAS:
Vincent and I are getting Billy.

Martha just looks at him, puzzled.

THOMAS:
We're getting official custody. It's something we've been working on for a while now.

MARTHA:
Billy will be living with you?

THOMAS:
Yes. It was June's idea, actually.

MARTHA:
She doesn't want him any more?

THOMAS:
She says she's not a very good parent. And I guess she wants to pursue her music. Of course, she can spend all the time with Billy she wants.

MARTHA:
I don't know what to say. I didn't know something like that was allowed.

THOMAS:
We both know Dad's going to flip out when he hears. I'm hoping you can be a buffer for that by breaking the news to him on the cruise.

VINCENT:
May I say something? Martha, you and I get along pretty well,

I think, and I want you to know that we've all given this a good deal of thought. The primary reason we're doing this is for Billy. With two of us in the home, he'll always have someone to be there for him.

> THOMAS:

I'm sure June will be over for dinner and visiting a lot. He'll have three parents, is what it amounts, too. We're all very excited about this. We know it's best for Billy.

> VINCENT:

I've been reading Dr. Spock.

> EMILY:

Change the subject, he's coming down.

George comes downstairs.

> GEORGE:

Emily! Come give your old man a hug.

Emily is taken aback by the greeting.

> EMILY:

Hi, Dad.

> GEORGE:

You heard me.

She moves to him, and they awkwardly embrace.

> GEORGE:

I know how busy you are, thanks for being here.

> EMILY:

Thomas wouldn't take no for an answer.

GEORGE:
Good for you, son. Family wouldn't be complete without you. What is it you used to say? "I want to be a falimy when I grow up!"

Emily speaks to the audience.

EMILY (TO AUDIENCE):
Something pops out of your mouth when you're seven, and it follows you to your grave.

MARTHA:
Weren't you able to sleep, dear?

GEORGE:
Don't want to sleep through the most important holiday of my lifetime! I can stay in bed all day tomorrow if it comes to that. I like your costume.

MARTHA:
She's America's first playwright.

GEORGE:
Mercy Otis Warren. Sister of James Otis.

EMILY:
I'm impressed.

GEORGE:
"No taxation without representation!" His law clerk, Samuel Adams, took that little proposition considerably farther than Otis intended. If I remember correctly, Otis went crazy when the fighting started, and they had to carry him out of Boston in a strait jacket.

EMILY:
A bit exaggerated, perhaps.

GEORGE (IGNORING THIS):
Otis spent the entire revolution in exile. He burned his life's work, he was so depressed about the violence. That's why we know so little about him. John Adams called him the First Patriot. You're not the only historian in the family, young lady.

EMILY:
Very good.

GEORGE:
After the revolution, they threw a James Otis Day for him in Boston, and at the celebration Otis saw Hamilton and others dancing the minuet. He thought they were behaving like a bunch of English aristocrats! Depressed him all over again. I think that's when he decided to burn all his papers. Mercy was editing them at the time.

EMILY:
There's some controversy about some of that.

Martha senses potential conflict and intervenes.

MARTHA:
Emily, let me give you the grand tour.

GEORGE:
Now mother, just relax. There's lots of time for grand tours.

MARTHA:
You're not going to start an argument about history, are you?

GEORGE:
No, I'm not starting an argument about anything. Emily, tell her.

EMILY (TENTATIVELY):
We're fine, Mom.

GEORGE (TO EMILY):
Now come with me.

He takes her hand and starts toward the stairs. Emily isn't sure what is going on and neither is anyone else.

MARTHA:
George?

GEORGE:
We'll be back before it's time to go. I'm sure you all can amuse yourselves.

THOMAS:
Dad, what's going on?

GEORGE:
Will everyone just relax, for God's sake?

They have started up the stairs.

EMILY:
Mom, it's okay.

Everyone watches them move up the stairs and out of sight.

VINCENT (TO THE AUDIENCE):
I love it when people act unpredictably! We all get in such ruts, don't you think?

THOMAS:
What's he doing?

MARTHA:
I have no idea.

THOMAS:
This is really weird, Mom.

VINCENT:
I think he's on a roll, and we should all just go along with it.

THOMAS:
You haven't been around him long enough to know what you're talking about.

MARTHA:
Maybe he just needs to talk to her alone.

VINCENT:
Exactly. Why do you always have to think the worst?

THOMAS:
Because those two are stubborn as hell and have the same argument every time they get together.

MARTHA:
And I for one refuse to sit here and get upset by it.

She starts away.

THOMAS:
Where are you going?

MARTHA:
I'm getting a head start on dinner.

She moves toward the kitchen, speaking to the audience:

MARTHA (TO AUDIENCE):
The glass is half-empty or it's half-full. It's completely up to you.

She exits.

THOMAS:
You don't know their history. This is definitely out of character.

VINCENT:
So what are you going to do? Sit here and wait for blood to come flowing down the stairs?

THOMAS:
That's not funny.

VINCENT:
I do detect something of a self-fulfilling prophecy in this family.

THOMAS:
You don't have any foundation for what you're saying. Let's change the subject.

VINCENT:
Okay. How about doing me a favor?

THOMAS:
What?

VINCENT:
Listen to my monologue. I need an audience.

CROSS FADE to bedroom upstairs.

GEORGE:
I need to lie down a minute.

He stretches out on the bed.

EMILY:
Dad, are you all right?

GEORGE:
Not exactly.

EMILY:
What's the problem?

GEORGE:
That's what I want to talk to you about.

EMILY:
Okay.

GEORGE:
We've had our differences, I realize, ever since you went to Berkeley. Before, I suppose, since high school. I just want you to know there's something I respect about you very much.

EMILY (ON HER GUARD)
And what's that?

GEORGE:
Your intellect.

EMILY:
You think I'm a stupid bleeding-heart liberal.

GEORGE:
That has more to do with values than intellect.

EMILY:
I'm not sure I understand the distinction in this case.

GEORGE:
Your values make you ask the wrong questions.

EMILY:
I see. Dad, if you brought me up here to try and change my value system.

GEORGE:
I didn't.

EMILY:
I almost didn't come here, to avoid this very conversation. I don't know why you can't just leave it alone.

GEORGE:
Have I said anything about Berkeley?

EMILY:
Surely you think that's where my values went wrong.

GEORGE:
Of course I do. Because they did. But I didn't bring it up, you did.

EMILY:
What kind of bullshit is that?

GEORGE:
All that education and you talk like a longshoreman. Excuse me, longshore person.

She starts for the stairs.

EMILY:
I'm not doing this, Dad.

George sits up, which takes some effort.

GEORGE:
Wait a minute.

EMILY:
I don't want to fight with you about college or the sixties or anything else. End of conversation.

She's heading out when she is stopped by what he says next.

GEORGE:
Damn it, Emily, I'm sick!

She turns to him.

GEORGE:
It's serious. I don't want your mother to know.

Emily slowly comes back into the room.

EMILY:
What's wrong with you?

GEORGE:
What isn't?

EMILY
Dad?

GEORGE:
You ready for this? One, I have cancer. Two, early Alzheimer's.

EMILY:
Dad, my God ...

GEORGE:
The double whammy.

EMILY
Have you started chemo?

GEORGE:
I will not be a guinea pig.

EMILY:
You're not having any kind of treatment?

GEORGE:
You saw what happened to your Uncle Henry. The cure is worse than the disease. Three months ago, they gave me six months. I think it's going to be less.

EMILY:
You haven't told anyone?

GEORGE:
No.

EMILY:
Why me?

GEORGE:
Because you're the only one in the family who can keep your head. I'm not going through what Henry went through, I can promise you that. I'm doing it myself first. I've been reading up on how to do that. I have to take care of business before my mind goes.

EMILY:
Dad, I'm so sorry.

GEORGE:
No tears, Emily. That's another reason I'm telling you. I haven't seen you cry since the fourth or fifth grade.

EMILY:
First time someone's complimented me on that particular character defect.

GEORGE:
Keeping control of your emotions is not a character defect.

EMILY:
So what you're telling me is, you're going to do it yourself?

GEORGE:
Yes.

EMILY:
How?

GEORGE:
With pills, liquor and a bag. It's as painless and clean as it gets.

EMILY:
Have you talked to your doctor about this?

GEORGE:
Of course not. He'd try to talk me out of it, if he didn't report me to the police. You fail at something like this, and they throw you in jail.

EMILY:
I see. So when is this going to happen?

GEORGE:
I was planning it right after the cruise. Only now I'm not sure I have that long. I'm already having mental lapses. If I wait too long ...

A silence.

EMILY:
There must be an easier way.

GEORGE:
I should be able to get a pill from my doctor. I've lived a long, full life. Try to find a doctor who will help you die.

EMILY
So what are you going to do?

GEORGE:
Believe me, I've thought a lot about the best way to do it. Do I do it alone and let someone discover me? Do I do it here, or would that make it unbearable for your mother to keep living here? So then do I get a motel room or what? And the more I think about it, the more I get angry that it has to be so complicated. A man dies, for Christ's sake. It's inevitable. It's the most natural thing in the world. So why can't this be as natural an event as a birth?

EMILY:
If it could happen any way you want, how would it be?

GEORGE:
I've thought about that, too. I'd have all of you around me. You'd respect my decision to do it this way. It would be like a celebration, like a wake, I suppose, and then we'd all say goodnight, goodbye, and I'd fall asleep and that would be that.

EMILY:
Dad, that's beautiful.

GEORGE:
Can you imagine your mother going along with that? Thomas would be even worse.

EMILY:
Have you thought about telling them what you want? Maybe they'll surprise you.

GEORGE:
I wouldn't know where to begin.

EMILY:
Just tell them what you told me. And tell them how you would like it to be.

A pause.

EMILY:
I could tell them, if you'd like.

GEORGE:
You'd do that, wouldn't you?

EMILY:
Of course I would.

GEORGE:
They say Indian chiefs would just walk into the woods and die when it was time. I think they had the right idea.

EMILY:
Talk to Mom. She needs to know what you're going through.

GEORGE:
I don't want a hysterical woman on my hands.

EMILY:
Give her the chance to surprise you. She's a very strong woman. And a very practical one. She saw what Uncle Henry went through, the same as you. She'll understand why you're doing this.

CROSS FADE to downstairs. Vincent is rehearsing his show, as Thomas listens.

VINCENT:
"...to institute a new kind of Family, laying its foundation on such principles and organizing its authority in such form, as to them seem most likely to effect the Safety and Welfare of the children. Such has been the patient sufferance of many men and women today, and such is now the necessity that constrains them to alter their former concept of Family."

He moves his focus from Thomas to the audience.

VINCENT:
"Prudence, indeed, would dictate that a definition of Family long established should not be changed for light and transient causes; and accordingly all experience hath shewn that humankind are more disposed to suffer, while evils are sufferable, than to right themselves by abolishing the forms of Family to which they are accustomed. But when a long train of atrocities and dysfunctions, pursuing invariably the same result, evinces a pattern to expose the children to unbearable suffering and insecurity, it is their right, it is their duty, to throw off such a definition of Family, and to provide new kinds of families for the well-being of the children."

George and Emily come downstairs.

GEORGE:
What the hell are you babbling about, Vincent?

VINCENT: (QUICKLY, TO AUDIENCE)
To be continued.

EMILY:
Where's Mom?

THOMAS:
In the kitchen.

Emily exits to fetch Martha.

GEORGE:
New kinds of families? Seriously, what was that about?

THOMAS:
Vincent was rehearsing for his little skit tonight.

VINCENT (TO AUDIENCE):
"His little skit"!

GEORGE:
About family values?

THOMAS:
Dad, it's nothing. I think we'd better get going.

GEORGE:
We've got lots of time.

THOMAS:
I'm sure traffic will be a nightmare.

Emily and Martha return.

EMILY:
Dad wants to have a family meeting.

THOMAS:
A what?

EMILY:
Family meeting. He has something to tell us.

MARTHA:
George?

GEORGE:
She's right, mother.

VINCENT:
In that case, if you will excuse me...

THOMAS:
You can stay.

There is a silence, while everyone looks to see what George will do.

GEORGE:
Sit down and relax, Vincent. All of you. This won't take long.

Everyone gets comfortable. There is tension in the room: George has never called "a family meeting" before.

GEORGE:
Well. This isn't going to be as easy as I thought.

EMILY:
You're doing fine.

MARTHA:
Emily, do you know what's going on here?

GEORGE:
Yes, she does, mother. I told her because I knew she's the only one in the family who wouldn't go into hysterics.

MARTHA:
What on earth are you talking about? I know you've been keeping something from me. What is it? George?

GEORGE:
Just calm down.

MARTHA:
I want to know what's going on here!

GEORGE:
I can't tell you while you're talking!

EMILY:
Dad, take it easy.

MARTHA:
George?

EMILY:
Mom, let him tell it his way.

A pause.

GEORGE:
Christ, what a mess.

EMILY:
Take your time.

A pause.

GEORGE:
I have cancer. Three months ago, they gave me six months to live.

Martha puts a hand over her mouth. Thomas stares in disbelief. Vincent is calm.

GEORGE:
I think that assessment was optimistic. Because I also have early Alzheimer's. The double whammy. Whatever I do, I need to do it while I still have my mind.

MARTHA:
Why didn't you tell me?

GEORGE:
I didn't want to upset you sooner than necessary. Any of you.

A silence.

GEORGE:
Look, this isn't any easier for me than it is for you. But I'm not going through what Henry went through. What would be the point if I'm demented? So I'm taking care of the situation myself.

A pause. No one knows what to say.

THOMAS:
Are you saying what I think you're saying?

GEORGE:
Yes, I am. And that part's been decided. No discussion.

VINCENT:
I think what you're doing is very brave.

EMILY:
So do I.

Martha and Thomas, on the other hand, look horrified.

GEORGE:
Upstairs, Emily asked me how it would happen if I could have my way. I told her I'd like all of you around me, that we'd have a kind of wake, and then I'd take the pills and liquor, and put the bag over my head, and go to sleep.

Martha suddenly gets up.

MARTHA:
Well, that's just fine for you, isn't it? You don't have to watch yourself twitch and groan and throw up and whatever else it is that happens!

She moves for the stairway.

GEORGE:
Mother!

Martha exits to the bedroom upstairs.

GEORGE (TO EMILY):
I told you this would happen.

EMILY:
Excuse me.

Emily goes upstairs to comfort Martha.

GEORGE:
Why the hell can't a man die as he pleases?

THOMAS:
Because it's selfish.

VINCENT:
Really?

THOMAS:
He's thinking only of himself.

VINCENT:
And who are you thinking of? I'm on your side, George, I think a man has the right to die any way he chooses.

THOMAS:
If you're determined to do that, why didn't you just go somewhere and do it? Why do you have to drag everyone else through the gory details?

Thomas gets up and goes to the bedroom upstairs. An awkward silence.

VINCENT:
Here's an unlikely coalition.

GEORGE:
What?

VINCENT:
I'm sorry. It struck me as funny.

GEORGE:
What did?

VINCENT:
The two of us. Being on the same side here.

A silence.

VINCENT:
Would you like to hear some of my show? I need the practice.

GEORGE:
Your show?

VINCENT:
How children have rights and families must be redefined to secure them.

GEORGE:
You can't redefine the family.

VINCENT:
Of course you can. Thomas and I are as good as married.

GEORGE:
That's absurd. Marriage is at the foundation of raising a family, a man and woman in holy bonding.

VINCENT:
We can do that, too.

GEORGE:
Not until science has men bearing children. The way this country's going, it'll probably happen. But that doesn't make it right.

VINCENT:
We can raise a child who's already been born.

GEORGE:
Adopt? They let you do that now?

VINCENT:
You're trying my patience here.

GEORGE:
Maybe they do. Wouldn't surprise me.

VINCENT:
Maybe you should just crawl off into the bushes and take care of business.

GEORGE:
You'd like that, I'm sure.

VINCENT:
That was uncalled for. I apologize. I truly do.

The stress has finally gotten to George. He sits with his head in his hands. A pause.

VINCENT:
I wish we could get along.

No response from George.

VINCENT:
I'd like to be a part of this family. I don't have one of my own. My parents are gone. My brother won't speak to me.

No reply.

VINCENT:
"I want to be a falimy when I grow up."

George looks up.

VINCENT:
It's a charming story. Thomas can't remember how old Emily was when she said it.

GEORGE:
Seven. Eight maybe. Thomas was always talking about how he wanted to be a policeman.

VINCENT:
A policeman! He never told me that part.

GEORGE:
And so Emily started saying, "I want to be a falimy when I grow up." She said it so often it could drive you crazy.

VINCENT:
I like it. "I want to be a falimy when I grow up."

GEORGE:
Your connection to this family, such as it is, is through lust.

VINCENT:
Why do straight people think gay people are sex fiends?

GEORGE:
I'll grant you one thing: I don't understand much of anything any more.

VINCENT:
I don't understand all that much myself. But I do understand this. That what happens between consenting adults in a bedroom doesn't have the earth-shattering influence on the state of the nation that some people think it does.

A pause.

GEORGE:
This isn't the way I wanted it to be.

VINCENT:
May I ask you a personal question?

No reply.

VINCENT:
What are you going to miss the most?

GEORGE:
What?

VINCENT:
What are you going to miss the most?

GEORGE:
Watching Billy grow up. But maybe that would end up being too painful. A boy needs two parents.

VINCENT:
Billy has two parents.

GEORGE:
I mean living together. A father, a mother, a family.

VINCENT:
He's getting two parents living together.
George stares at him.

GEORGE:
June's getting remarried?

VINCENT:
No.

GEORGE:
I don't understand.

VINCENT:
June doesn't think she's a good parent.

GEORGE:
No wonder, trying to raise a boy by herself. Going to a job, going to school. I have no idea why she decided to go to night school.

VINCENT:
She wants to be a musician. A jazz vocalist, piano player, something like that. It's so important to her that she's giving up Billy.

GEORGE:
What are you talking about?

VINCENT:
She's giving him to Thomas and I to raise. We're going to be the primary providers, the parents, for Billy. Of course, she'll be able to visit as often as she likes.

GEORGE:
You're getting Billy?

Vincent nods.

GEORGE:
You and Thomas?

Vincent nods.

VINCENT:
We're going to be a falimy.

George stares at him.

BLACKOUT. *Act One is over.*

ACT II

Scene 1

LIGHTS UP FULL to reveal: the same moment that ended Act One.

GEORGE:
You and Thomas?

Vincent nods.

VINCENT:
We're going to be a falimy.

George stares at him.

VINCENT:
I think we'll be excellent parents.

GEORGE:
But it's not quite the same as being husband and wife and a real family, is it?

VINCENT:
No, it's not the same, it's better. Because Thomas and I can give Billy a stable home.

A pause.

VINCENT:
I admit I'm nervous. I've been reading Dr. Spock.

GEORGE:
Dr. Spock. Maybe that's what happened. A whole generation of mothers took a pinko's advice on raising their children.

George stands up. He wearily starts for the kitchen.

VINCENT:
I had a fantasy you and Martha would live in a cottage behind our house.

George stops and turns to Vincent.

VINCENT:
I think the loss of grandparents, the loss of the extended family, is a great tragedy in American life.

GEORGE:
You do?

VINCENT:
Absolutely. You look surprised.

GEORGE:
I'm shocked, to be honest. Were you close to your grandparents?

VINCENT:
Very. To both of them. My grandfather told me things about my dad that I'd never have learned otherwise. It's a valuable perspective to have. Billy will lose so much, missing that.

A pause. George is studying him.

GEORGE:
I'm having a Ramos fizz. Care to join me?

VINCENT:
Normally it's early for me, but under the circumstances, yes. Nice of you to ask.

GEORGE:
I have the original recipe. I'll make a pitcher.

He exits, as Thomas comes downstairs.

VINCENT (TO AUDIENCE):
That turned out much better than I expected.

THOMAS:
What's going on?

VINCENT:
He's making Ramos fizzes. I told him. Thomas, I had to. He's so worried about Billy. We have to convince him this is the right thing to do.

THOMAS:
You'll never convince him of that.

VINCENT:
I think he's more reasonable than you think.

THOMAS:
On what evidence do you say that?

VINCENT:
His world is changing. It's ending actually. That must be a terrible thing to go through. Maybe we'll feel the same way when we're his age.

THOMAS:
The man is a homophobe.

VINCENT:
He's also dying.

THOMAS:
Don't lecture me on dying. I watched one of my best friends die, moment by moment.

VINCENT:
I know you did, Thomas.

THOMAS:
Frank fought back to his last breath, he found joy beyond my comprehension in what life was left to him. He was so brave!

Emily comes downstairs.

EMILY:
Mom's taking a nap. Where's Dad?

THOMAS:
Finally making his Ramos fizzes.

EMILY:
Are we having a wake?

THOMAS:
Ask Vincent. He and Dad have become bosom buddies. (To Vincent) I can't believe you told him.

VINCENT:
It was spontaneous. A gut feeling it was the right thing to do. Maybe you had to be there.

THOMAS:
When he gets some liquor in him, we'll never hear the end of it.

VINCENT:
Lighten up. Give your old man a break, I think he's going to surprise you. I'll see if he needs any help. (To audience, on his way out) Falimies!

Vincent exits.

THOMAS:
I don't believe this.

EMILY:
Try to go with the flow. It's all you can do.

THOMAS:
How can you defend him?

EMILY:
I think it's his right to choose how he dies.

THOMAS:
At our expense?

EMILY:
He's been keeping it from everyone, as a matter of fact. I'm the one who suggested telling you. I thought you had a right to know. If I knew how you were going to handle it...

THOMAS:
Mom's not taking it any better than I am.

EMILY:
She was shocked, but she's stronger than any of us. Mom will be fine.

THOMAS:
So what are we supposed to do now? Get drunk with him and call it a wake?

EMILY:
We're going with the flow.

THOMAS:
What about the parade?

EMILY:
I guess we play it by ear.

George and Vincent return with a pitcher of Ramos fizzes and glasses.

VINCENT:
Who's ready for a Ramos fizz?

THOMAS:
It's a little early, isn't it?

VINCENT:
It is the Bicentennial.

GEORGE:
Who am I pouring for?

EMILY:
I'll have one.

GEORGE:
Thomas?

THOMAS:
Too early for me.

VINCENT ("PARTY POOPER"):
You sure?

THOMAS:
Positive.

GEORGE:
Where's Martha?

EMILY:
Upstairs napping.

GEORGE:
I shouldn't have told her.

THOMAS:
I don't think you should've told any of us.

GEORGE:
(to Emily) See there? (To Thomas) Why not?

THOMAS:
I was expressing my opinion. I don't want to start an argument.

EMILY:
Good idea.

GEORGE:
What's wrong with a debate? If you don't have the courage of your convictions, where are you?

THOMAS:
We have never had a debate in this family. We have arguments, and this doesn't seem like the time or place.

GEORGE:
Better take advantage of me while you can.

THOMAS:
Dad, for Christ's sake …

GEORGE:
What? I'm dying, goddamn it! You think I like doing this?

THOMAS:
I think you like...

A pause.

GEORGE:
Say it.

THOMAS: (TO AUDIENCE)
He's determined to pick a fight with me.

GEORGE:
Say it!

THOMAS:
I think you like the notoriety of this.

GEORGE:
Notoriety.

EMILY: ("DON'T DO THIS")
Thomas...

GEORGE (TO AUDIENCE):
You raise a child, and what the hell happens? You try to give a child a sense of how the world works. If you stick your hand in fire, you get burned. If you cross the street without looking, you

have a chance of getting hit. But that's about all you can accomplish.

    VINCENT:
For the record, I don't think any of this has anything to do with wanting notoriety.

    THOMAS:
What do you know about it?

    VINCENT:
I know the man isn't doing this in order to amuse us with some kind of holiday fireworks.

    THOMAS:
What're you talking about? You don't plan on doing this today, do you? Jesus Christ!

    GEORGE:
No, I wasn't planning to.

    VINCENT:
I'm talking about the context of what he's going through. You said his motive was notoriety.

    THOMAS:
I was angry, okay? I didn't mean it the way it came out.

    GEORGE:
I know you didn't mean it, son.

A pause.

    GEORGE:
But why not today?

EMILY:
Dad?

GEORGE:
I feel like my own body has become a time bomb. So what the hell am I supposed to do about it? Something before my mind goes. So ... why not today?

THOMAS:
Great, Vincent, you and your big mouth.

VINCENT:
Whoa, Silver! Are you blaming me for something?

THOMAS:
You put the idea in his head.

GEORGE:
And not a bad one either.

EMILY:
Dad, don't pursue this unless you really mean it.

GEORGE:
I do mean it. I feel better having said so.

THOMAS:
You don't know what you're saying.

GEORGE:
I've been walking around like a deflated balloon. I feel like I've just gotten a jolt of helium.

A pause. Everyone just looks at him.

GEORGE:
The problem will be getting your mother to go along. I could use some help with that.

EMILY:
You're really serious about this?

GEORGE:
All of you are already here. That's the way I've wanted it to be ever since I decided. I just worry about Martha.

EMILY:
I can talk to her.

GEORGE:
I'd appreciate that. The sooner the better.

EMILY:
She's napping.

GEORGE:
Are you sure? I think she's escaping. Check on her, would you? I think she needs to be down here now.

EMILY:
Excuse me.

She starts away, speaking to the audience.

EMILY:
I have no doubts that he's serious.

She exits upstairs.

VINCEENT:
You're a remarkable man.

GEORGE:
Not much choice when you have to face facts.

THOMAS:
Oh, please.

Thomas goes upstairs.

VINCENT:
This is a side of Thomas I've never seen before.

GEORGE:
He's so damn thin-skinned.

CROSS FADE to upstairs. Emily sits on the edge of the bed.

MARTHA:
Is it time to go to the parade?

EMILY:
Not yet.

MARTHA:
Where's George?

EMILY:
Downstairs. How are you feeling?

MARTHA:
Worried about George. He won't go to a doctor.

EMILY:
He's afraid to. He saw what happened to Uncle Henry.

MARTHA:
I know. I don't blame him. Who would want to go through that?

EMILY:
Mom, he's not feeling well at all. I mean today, right now. Since all of us are already here, well, he's thinking maybe now is the time.

MARTHA:
The time?

THOMAS (ENTERING):
We can't let him go through with it.

EMILY:
Don't meddle in what you don't understand.

THOMAS:
Don't lecture me about "understanding!" I buried my oldest friend last year.

MARTHA:
Please don't fight.

EMILY:
I'm sorry. I just think Dad has the right to choose how he leaves us.

THOMAS:
Not when he's putting us through this.

MARTHA:
What would you do?

THOMAS:
I'd call the police.

EMILY:
Don't be ridiculous.

THOMAS:
He's a danger to himself. That's obvious, isn't it? His Alzheimer's more advanced than he thinks. He doesn't know what he's saying.

MARTHA:
I think he knows perfectly well.

THOMAS:
Mom, this is not like him. He's never been a coward.

EMILY:
He's not being a coward now.

MARTHA:
We don't feel how much pain he's in.

THOMAS:
You want to talk about pain? When Frank died last winter, that was pain. But he never gave up.

EMILY:
Thomas, it's not the same thing.

MARTHA:
I'd better see how he's doing.

She'll start downstairs.

THOMAS:
Frank faced death with so much courage. Why is Dad giving up? Why won't he fight it?

EMILY:
I don't know. But I think it's his right to.

CROSS FADE to downstairs, as Martha enters.

MARTHA:
George, how are you feeling?

GEORGE:
Better, under the circumstances. Did Emily talk to you?

MARTHA:
Yes, she did.

GEORGE:
Good. I feel relieved about making a decision. I think maybe the uncertainty was the worst part. Now I feel like I have a purpose again.

MARTHA:
What about the parade?

GEORGE:
They'll have to get along without us.

MARTHA:
You were looking forward to it.

GEORGE:
I've been looking forward to lots of things, mother. I know how much you were looking forward to the cruise.

MARTHA:
George, the cruise doesn't matter now.

GEORGE:
I need to know I'm in control, and that feeling is going fast. I have it right now, but I can't tell you if I'll have it tomorrow. I've always wanted everyone around me for this. And here you are.

Emily and Thomas have entered above.

THOMAS:
Am I the only one who is against this?

There is a silence. Vincent nods at him.

THOMAS:
Dad, for the last time, please see a doctor. Let me call an ambulance.

GEORGE:
I'm not going through what Henry went through.

THOMAS:
They're making progress in medical research all the time! Just because Uncle Henry went through hell doesn't mean you have to. They're always coming up with something new.

GEORGE:
Maybe you're right, but it's not a gamble I'm willing to take.

THOMAS:
Why won't you fight this, for Billy's sake?

GEORGE:
Don't think I haven't thought about it. But if I don't even recognize him ...

THOMAS:
You don't know that.

GEORGE:
Maybe I'm just too tired. Not just my health. Any of it. What America's become. It's not my world any more. I don't belong here.

A pause.

GEORGE:
Mother, you want a fizz?

MARTHA:
Yes, thank you.

GEORGE:
Thomas?

THOMAS:
No.

GEORGE: (MUSTERING ENERGY)
I thought we were having a wake here. Everyone looks so glum.

Everyone just looks at him.

GEORGE:
I think we should be celebrating the good times we've had. There were many of them, as I remember.

EMILY:
I remember lots of good times, too.

VINCENT:
I want to be a falimy when I grow up.

MARTHA:
You were so adorable when you came up with that.

EMILY:
Went downhill from there, didn't I?

MARTHA:
What do you mean?

EMILY:
I never quite reached that level of adoration again.

THOMAS:
That's ridiculous.

EMILY:
When was I the apple of anyone's eye again?

THOMAS:
When you got the scholarship to U Mass. I was damn proud of you then.

EMILY:
I don't think we want to get into that, Thomas.

GEORGE:
Why not?

EMILY:
Isn't it obvious?

MARTHA:
George, Emily's right.

GEORGE:
For God's sake, why is everybody so worried about everything? We still have freedom of speech in this family, same as in the country.

VINCENT (TO AUDIENCE):
More or less.

MARTHA:
Please, let's not talk about politics.

THOMAS:
I was just pointing out that Emily's life didn't end when she was seven, as far as being admired is concerned.

GEORGE:
U Mass was a hell of a lot better than Berkeley, I'll grant you that. At least she started going to classes again.

EMILY:
You stopped paying my bills at Berkeley. What choice did I have?

GEORGE:
I offered you the option of returning to class.

EMILY:
How could I attend class when there was a strike going on?

GEORGE:
You could have ignored it.

EMILY:
Strike-breaking was not an option.

GEORGE:
See there? I rest my case.

MARTHA:
Stop it! Both of you.

She moves forward to speak to the audience.

> MARTHA (TO AUDIENCE):
> The more we disagreed with him, the more stubborn he was going to get.

Martha moves quickly back into the scene.

> MARTHA:
> So how can we help out, George? Are you doing it down here or upstairs?

> GEORGE:
> I haven't gotten that far.

> MARTHA:
> If you're doing it, don't you think it's time to get ready? You're not going to be much use if you get drunk.

> THOMAS (TAKING MARTHA ASIDE):
> What are you doing? If he gets drunk, we can call the police.

> GEORGE:
> No conspiracies, Thomas!

He gets to his feet, and Emily goes to him.

> EMILY:
> Are you all right?

> GEORGE:
> Mother's right. I have to get my bag upstairs.

> EMILY:
> I'll get it. Tell me where.

GEORGE:
A blue canvas bag in the back of my closet.

THOMAS:
Anyone who helps him can be charged with murder.

GEORGE:
He's right.

EMILY
I'll cover my tracks.

Emily exits.

VINCENT:
Is there anything I can do?

GEORGE:
Keep Thomas from pestering me.

THOMAS:
Don't worry. It's obvious I can't stop you.

GEORGE:
Thank you. It's not the same as getting my family behind me, but it's better than nothing.

VINCENT:
You have a lot of support here.

GEORGE:
You surprise me, Vincent.

VINCENT:
Well, you've surprised me, too.

GEORGE:
I'm not condoning homosexuality.

VINCENT:
I'm not condoning Republicans.

MARTHA:
I don't want to hear anything about politics. George, you said you wanted to remember the good times. Maybe we should show some movies.

GEORGE:
I've got a better idea. We can tell stories.

VINCENT:
I love family stories.

GEORGE:
We have our share.

THOMAS:
Everyone's heard them a zillion times.

VINCENT:
I haven't. I'm sure there's many I've never heard.

CROSS FADE to Emily upstairs. She has the blue bag on the bed and has unzipped it. She is looking through its contents.

EMILY (TO AUDIENCE):
He'd done his homework. There was a pamphlet with instructions on how to use the pills, which would be crushed and mixed in apple sauce; and the liquor, mixed with fruit concentrate; and a large bag to fit over the head; and a large rubber band to secure it, all items of which were in the bag. There was a spoon, other utensils. No doubt about his making preparations for this. But looking at the contents in the bag,

understanding how much thought and work had already gone into this, suddenly my father's suicide became something more than an idea, a theory, and I felt myself having a change of heart.

CROSS FADE downstairs.

> GEORGE:
We shouldn't begin until Emily gets here. Maybe she's having trouble up there.

> VINCENT:
I'll check.

He starts for the stairs but meets Emily as she comes down and enters the room, carrying the blue bag.

> EMILY:
Here it is.

She gives the bag to George.

> MARTHA:
We thought we'd tell family stories.

> EMILY:
Dad, I'm having second thoughts about this.

> THOMAS:
Thank God!

> GEORGE:
Don't disappoint me here.

> EMILY:
So much can go wrong that would be painful for you.

GEORGE:
Nothing will go wrong. I have a pamphlet you can read.

EMILY:
I glanced at it.

GEORGE:
You snooped in my bag? Can't I trust anybody around here?

THOMAS:
Emily's right. A lot can go wrong here, Dad.

GEORGE:
Then I'll do the goddamn thing by myself.

He starts unsteadily for the stairs.

MARTHA:
George, we're going to tell family stories.

GEORGE:
You have to have a goddamn family to do that.

The doorbell rings. For a moment, everyone stops and looks at the door. No one is expected.

THOMAS:
I'll get it.

He opens the door and June steps in.

JUNE:
Sorry to come without calling first. Can we go somewhere and talk?

But George has seen her.

GEORGE:
June! Get yourself in here!

MARTHA:
George, don't start something.

GEORGE:
What's this I hear about you abandoning motherhood?

JUNE:
What's going on?

THOMAS:
Bad timing, really bad timing.

GEORGE:
Tell me I heard wrong!

JUNE:
Is he all right?

THOMAS:
Not by a long shot.

GEORGE:
Will you get in here?

June moves into the room, with Thomas following.

JUNE:
If I'm interrupting something …"

VINCENT:
June, would you like a Ramos fizz? Believe me, it will help.

JUNE:
I can't stay. I just need to talk to Thomas a minute.

GEORGE:
You're avoiding the question. Are you giving up Billy or not?

Everyone is waiting for her answer.

JUNE:
We need to change the plan.

THOMAS:
Jesus Christ.

JUNE:
Thomas, something's come up.

VINCENT:
This isn't fair.

JUNE:
I'm not backing out. I have a chance to tour with a band. I want to wait until fall.

GEORGE:
You know in your heart it's wrong to give up your child. I'm proud of you.

JUNE (TO THOMAS):
Can we go somewhere and talk?

THOMAS:
We damn well better. Vincent?

VINCENT (TO MARTHA):
Are you going to be okay?

MARTHA:
I'll be fine.

GEORGE:
People can't move their children around like real estate. What the hell happened to this country?

THOMAS (TO MARTHA):
We'll be back as soon as we can.

Thomas, Vincent and June exit.

GEORGE:
She doesn't want to do this. They're twisting her arm. I'm ashamed to have a son who'd do a thing like that.

EMILY:
I think it really was her idea, Dad.

GEORGE:
Sounds to me like she's changed her mind.

EMILY:
I'm sure it's not an easy decision for her.

George starts again for the stairs, moving unsteadily, and Martha hurries to support him.

MARTHA:
What do you think you're doing?

GEORGE:
You know damn well what I'm doing.

MARTHA:
You can't do something like this out of spite.

GEORGE:
I can do it any goddamn way I choose to do it. Get out of my way.

MARTHA:
George, please!

GEORGE:
Leave me alone!

Martha, close to losing it, sits down.

EMILY:
Dad, you're not being fair. You don't have to cause this much hurt.

George stops and turns into the room. We sense he knows she's right but is too proud to admit it.

EMILY:
Do it bravely, not cruelly.

GEORGE:
Who's being cruel here? Is it too much to ask for the support of my family?

Vincent steps out to address the audience, continuing his one-man show.

VINCENT (TO AUDIENCE):
"The history of the present Family in the United States is a history of repeated injuries and usurpations, all having in direct object the establishment of absolute Disregard for the well-being and security of children. To prove this, let Facts be submitted to a candid world."

GEORGE:
I wanted family support and didn't get it. You turned on me

yourself.

EMILY:
I apologize for that. Seeing what was in the bag made it seem more real to me than before. I panicked for a minute.

VINCENT (TO AUDIENCE):
"Over half the marriages in the United States end in divorce; almost one in three divorced adults cites abuse as the reason for termination;"

EMILY:
This isn't easy for any of us, Dad.

VINCENT (TO AUDIENCE):
"One-quarter of the violent crimes in the U.S. is wife assault;"

GEORGE:
Please don't cry, mother. I need you to be strong now.

MARTHA:
I don't think I have any strength left.

George moves to Martha.

VINCENT (TO AUDIENCE):
"A woman is physically abused in this country every nine seconds;"

GEORGE:
Give me your hand.

Martha does. George helps her to her feet.

VINCENT (TO AUDIENCE):
"Two-thirds of the attacks are by someone she knows, often a husband or boyfriend;"

GEORGE:
I'm asking you to come upstairs with me.

MARTHA:
Are you sure this is the only way?

GEORGE:
Positive.

VINCENT (TO AUDIENCE):
"Sixty percent of battered women are beaten while they are pregnant;"

MARTHA:
Don't you want to wait and see if June changes her mind?

GEORGE:
I wish I could wait for a lot of things. But I can't.

VINCENT (TO AUDIENCE):
"Forty-two percent of murdered women are killed by their intimate male partners;"

GEORGE:
There're no good choices here, mother. This is the best one we have.

VINCENT (TO AUDIENCE):
"One in six female rape victims is under the age of 12; one-fifth of these have been raped by their fathers;"

GEORGE:
Will you come upstairs with me?

MARTHA:
Of course, I will.

They start upstairs together, moving slowly.

VINCENT (TO AUDIENCE):
"By conservative estimates, one in three girls is sexually abused by age 18, one in four by age 14;"

EMILY:
Can't I come?

VINCENT (TO AUDIENCE):
"Approximately one in six boys is sexually abused by age 16;"

GEORGE:
I thought you didn't approve.

EMILY:
I was scared for a minute, Dad. Don't hold it against me.

GEORGE:
Then come along if you like.

They head slowly for the stairs, the pace determined by George, who is in clear physical pain.

VINCENT (TO AUDIENCE):
"The average age of entry into prostitution is 13; there are half a million adolescent prostitutes in the United States;"

MARTHA:
Are you sure you can make it up the stairs? We can do it down here.

GEORGE:
I think I'd like to be in my own bed. Unless you don't

approve. I can see how you wouldn't.

MARTHA:
I'd rather do it down here, George.

GEORGE:
Then down here it is.

They will move slowly back to the divan.

VINCENT (TO AUDIENCE):
"So destructive are these oppressions to the welfare of children, and so linked are they to the assumptions of traditional family values, that we must now declare a new and independent kind of Family for the raising and nurturing of our children;"

GEORGE:
I've already crushed up the pills. I just have to mix them in the apple sauce. And pour the concentrate in the vodka. Maybe you could do that for me, Emily.

EMILY:
Of course.

She'll go to the divan, open the bag and begin the preparations.

VINCENT (TO AUDIENCE):
"In behalf of our children, we therefore and hereby publish and declare that we hold no further allegiance to traditional family values and replace them with more stable values stemming from a broader concept of Family, in which parents may be any two adults committed and pledged to the rearing of children;"

MARTHA:
Here we are.

She helps George onto the divan. Emily is preparing the food and drink.

GEORGE:
I should've done this yesterday.

MARTHA:
I'm glad you waited.

EMILY:
I wouldn't have seen you if you'd done that.

VINCENT (TO AUDIENCE):
"That the biological mother need not be one of these nurturing parents;"

GEORGE:
How's it coming?

EMILY:
Almost ready.

GEORGE:
The head bag should be in there. With a rubber band.

EMILY:
I found it.

MARTHA:
I hate seeing you in pain.

GEORGE:
This is going to be a great relief, mother. Emily?

EMILY:
Okay. What do you do first?

GEORGE:
The apple sauce.

Emily hands George the jar of applesauce into which she has mixed the crushed pills. She hands him a spoon. He eats the applesauce.

VINCENT (TO AUDIENCE):
"That these parents may include homosexual couples and lesbian couples, whether ritually married or not;"

MARTHA:
A part of me wants to do this with you.

GEORGE:
Don't be ridiculous. You'll live to be ninety.

George finishes the apple sauce.

GEORGE:
Now the other.

Emily gives him the bottle of vodka, into which the concentrate has been poured. George drinks it.

VINCENT (TO AUDIENCE):
"And that no criteria for parenthood are appropriate except commitment to the welfare of the children and to learning the skills necessary for securing same;"

GEORGE:
The bag.

Emily helps put the bag over George's head, securing it with a rubber band. Both women help him stretch out on the divan.

MARTHA:
I'm taking your hand, George. You give me a yank if

something goes wrong and you want the bag removed. Do you understand me?

George shakes his head and speaks through the bag, "I hear you!" Then he stretches out, getting comfortable.

VINCENT (TO AUDIENCE):
"Signed under oath, July 4, 1976."

Vincent exits.

A pause. Both women sit with George, Martha holding his hand.

EMILY:
Dad, I need to tell you something I should've said a long time ago. Remember when you were on the road, how you used to take me on business trips sometimes? I must've been 9 or 10. I especially remember a trip we took to Phoenix, and afterwards we drove to the Grand Canyon. We always stopped at the historical markers and you'd read them to me and explain more about the history. You seemed to know everything about the history of where we were, no matter where we went. I think it was those trips that turned me into an historian. Those are wonderful memories. What I'm trying to say is, it wasn't easy for us during the sixties, it wasn't an easy time for anybody, and somehow we built this wall between us, we found differences that we had as adults that were irrelevant when I was Daddy's Girl, going on business trips with you, worshiping you, really ... we just got off track and somehow our differences began to outweigh the rest. I just want you to know that I cherish those memories. I always have. I always will. I love you, Dad.

George suddenly jerks the hand Martha holds. The free hand pulls at the bag as he makes loud noises of fear.

EMILY
Call 911! Now, Martha, 911!

Martha hurries to the phone. Emily helps George remove the bag, taking charge.

LIGHTS FADE TO BLACKOUT.

Scene 2

LIGHTS UP. Living room. A YEAR LATER, July 4, 1977.

Thomas and June face the audience, looking out a window to the front yard. Thomas, and everyone else, wears street clothes now.

JUNE:
He's grown so much!

THOMAS:
Tell me about it.

JUNE:
He really likes Vincent, doesn't he?

THOMAS:
Vincent is incredible. He's like a natural mother and an ideal dad combined. You know what he's doing? Learning to play softball. He's not naturally athletic at all, but he wants to be able to play catch with the kid and all the rest, so he enrolled in this softball class at the Y, and he's on a team and everything. He's so bad at it! But he doesn't quit, I'll hand that to him.

JUNE:
He's so devoted to being a parent.

THOMAS:
Totally. He quit his job.

JUNE:
Can you two afford that?

THOMAS:
He's consulting out of the house. He has as much work as he wants.

JUNE:
I'm glad things are turning out so well for you.

THOMAS:
How about you? How'd you like touring Europe?

JUNE:
It was grueling, and I missed Billy terribly, of course. Sending photos really helped me.

THOMAS:
I'm amazed they ever caught up with you. So you're home for a while?

JUNE:
Until we have to promote the album. Then it's back on the road

THOMAS:
Things are working out for you, too, then.

JUNE:
He sees us. (She waves) Hi, Billy! (She blows him a kiss) Well, I guess we'd better get going.

THOMAS:
You can have him a day longer if you like.

JUNE:
We'll see how it goes. Can I give you a call?

THOMAS:
Of course.

They embrace.

> JUNE:
> We did something great having Billy, didn't we?

> THOMAS:
> Yes, we did.

> JUNE:
> What time are you going to the cemetery?

> THOMAS:
> Twoish.

> JUNE:
> We'll meet you there.

> THOMAS:
> That'd be great.

> JUNE:
> Thanks again for everything.

She kisses him on the cheek and exits out the front door. Martha comes downstairs from the bedroom.

> MARTHA:
> Has June left yet?

> THOMAS:
> She's just leaving. You can catch her if you hurry.

Martha hurries out the front door, as Emily enters from the den.

> EMILY:
> June take Billy?

THOMAS:
They're just leaving.

EMILY:
How long before we go to the cemetery?

THOMAS:
A couple hours. Two, I think Mom said.

EMILY:
It seems like more than a year to me.

THOMAS:
I know what you mean.

EMILY:
He would've liked how Billy is turning out.

THOMAS:
Maybe.

Vincent enters through the front door.

VINCENT:
Did you try to convince her to take him another day?

THOMAS:
I did. She's going to call later. And meet us at the cemetery, too.

VINCENT (TO EMILY):
We need a break.

EMILY:
I can imagine.

VINCENT:
Not that being a mother isn't the most delightful experience of my life. I just need the battery recharged now and then.

EMILY:
You two are great with him. I think Dad would have seen it and been proud.

VINCENT:
I think he would have, too.

THOMAS:
It's nice to think so.

VINCENT:
Ever the pessimist. (He gives Thomas a hug.) I love you anyway.

THOMAS:
I don't feel like there's closure. I leave, scared to death we're not getting Billy after all and when I come home, he's in the emergency room.

EMILY:
It was an ugly, difficult time - but before it was over, he had that incredible time with Billy at Disneyland. I focus on that.

THOMAS:
Half the time, he didn't know who Billy was.

EMILY
But Billy always knew who grandpa was.

Martha enters the front door.

MARTHA:
Now that that's taken care of, I have an announcement

to make.

The others exchange surprised glances, wondering what's up.

> MARTHA:
> I'm leaving on a cruise next week.
>
> THOMAS:
> Mom, that's great.
>
> EMILY:
> How long will you be gone?
>
> MARTHA:
> A year.
>
> THOMAS:
> A year!
>
> EMILY:
> Where on earth are you going?
>
> MARTHA:
> Around the world. I'm taking my time. George planned the whole itinerary for me.

George enters, beaming at her.

> MARTHA:
> After touring the Caribbean, I go to England and spend three months in London. Then Paris, Rome.
>
> EMILY:
> Dad planned everything out?
>
> GEORGE (TO AUDIENCE):
> My last coherent act of any complexity.

THOMAS:
Why didn't you tell us before?

MARTHA:
I hadn't made up my mind whether to do it. It took me all this time to decide.

EMILY:
Is someone renting the condo?

MARTHA:
I'm selling it.

GEORGE (TO AUDIENCE):
I thought she'd've done it before now, to tell the truth.

MARTHA:
It's so much more room than I need.

VINCENT:
Do you know where you're moving?

MARTHA:
I'll worry about that when I get back.

VINCENT:
I have a suggestion. We talked about it, Thomas.

THOMAS:
You tell her. (To audience) Vincent feels much stronger about this than I do.

VINCENT:
We need a larger place as well, so why don't you move in with us?

MARTHA:
Heavens, I couldn't do that.

VINCENT:
Please think about it.

Vincent stares at Thomas.

VINCENT (TO AUDIENCE):
I was going to stare at him until he spoke up!

He stares at Thomas some more.

THOMAS:
We were thinking of looking for a house with a cottage behind it, or maybe an apartment attached. Something like that. You wouldn't have to be under foot.

VINCENT (TO AUDIENCE):
A point on which he would not compromise.

MARTHA:
At least that wouldn't be like living in the same house. I need my space as much as you do.

VINCENT:
Billy would love having you so close.

EMILY:
What a great idea.

GEORGE (TO AUDIENCE):
She took the words right out of my mouth.

EMILY:
Good for you guys.

VINCENT (TO AUDIENCE):
"Guys!" Isn't she sweet?

THOMAS:
No need to decide now.

VINCENT:
You can think about it in London, Rome, Paris! I'm already jealous.

MARTHA:
And I will think about it. So who's ready for lunch?

Everyone exits to the kitchen, and George speaks to the audience.

GEORGE (TO AUDIENCE):
For the record, the cure was worse than the disease. But what a tradeoff! We took Billy to Disneyland, staying in the hotel there, and he and I didn't miss a ride. I can still hear his screams of joy! After that, it didn't matter what happened ... as long as I could hear his joy ... which I did ... and still do ...

He is lying on the divan. He closes his eyes. The LIGHTS SLOWLY FADE as we hear:

VINCENT (RECORDED VOICE):
"We hold these truths to be self-evident, that all children are created equal, that they are endowed by their Creator with certain unalienable rights, that among these are Life, Shelter, Security, Education, and Nurturing. That to secure these rights, Families are instituted among men and women..."

The lights have faded slowly to BLACKOUT. The play is over.

THE OLD BEATNIK

CAST:
LOLA-80 ... Lola in her 80s, bohemian, unreformed Beat poet, early dementia
LOLA-20/30/40... Lola when younger
EVELYN ... Lola's granddaughter, 20s
FRANK ... Young Lola's boyfriend, father of Lola's child, Evelyn's mother, 20-30s
PAUL ... Evelyn's fiancée, 30s

SET:
Split set ... one half contemporary Starbucks, one half 1950s coffee house

TIME:
Present and past as indicated

ACT I

Scene 1

Split stage: left, a contemporary Starbucks; right, a 1950s era coffeehouse. AT RISE: focus on LOLA-20 in coffeehouse, reading a poem. Dressed in black. It is 1954.

LOLA-20

O America / if Paris had kept his cock in his pants / would a thousand ships never have launched?

CROSSFADE to Starbucks. EVELYN alone at a table, on her cell phone. Her attire reveals wealth. It is 2015.

Baristas, customers, represented by cardboard figures. Or not at all.

EVELYN

I don't think she's coming, Paul. You might as well join me....You know how on again, off again, she was about meeting me. ...We're here, we might as well make the best of it....--Wait a minute. I think she just came in.

On Lola-20 in coffeehouse.

LOLA-20

O America / if you had kept your cock in your pants / would you have built your city not on a hill but in the valley? / If you had kept your cock in your pants, / would you have settled for a destiny less than manifest?

In Starbucks. Lola-80 slowly approaches Evelyn's table. The black clothes have turned shabby. One might guess she is homeless, though she isn't.

EVELYN
Lola?

LOLA-80
Hello. Are you the one I'm supposed to meet?

EVELYN
I'm Evelyn.

LOLA-80
Did we talk on the phone?

EVELYN
Several times.

LOLA-80
Who are you again?

EVELYN
Angel's daughter. I'm your granddaughter.

LOLA-80
My granddaughter. Isn't that something?

EVELYN
I'd almost given up on you.

LOLA-80
I was standing out there for the longest time. I had no idea what I was doing here. I've never been inside a Starbucks before. I avoid them. Then I saw you through the window. You looked familiar.

EVELYN
You've never been to Starbucks? Are you serious?

LOLA-80
I'm always serious. Places like this frighten me. I don't want to become infected.

EVELYN
I'm sure there's no danger. They keep it very clean.

LOLA-80
Spiritually infected. Abandon my values for convenience. Look at this place. It's antiseptic. It's like a waiting room in a hospital. Who would want to get it on here?
  (singing)
Why don't we do it in the road?

EVELYN
Grandma!

Lola-80 sits down.

LOLA-80
Grandma. I've never been called that before.

EVELYN
It just came out. I'm sorry if--

LOLA-80
Never apologize for speaking the truth. What was your name again?

EVELYN
Evelyn.

LOLA-80
Right. My granddaughter.

EVELYN
Yes.

LOLA-80
Isn't that something?

EVELYN
Yes, it is.

LOLA-80
My granddaughter. You found me.

On Lola-20 in coffeehouse.

LOLA-20
O America / if you keep your cock in your pants, / will our sordid history finally come to an end? / Let me tell you the sad truth, America: / your history has been driven by the one-eyed tyrant between your legs.

In Starbucks.

EVELYN
Everybody told me you were dead. I only learned otherwise last year after mom died.

LOLA-80
At my age I sometimes feel dead.

EVELYN
Paul googled you. My fiancée. He was looking if you had any other books.

LOLA-80
Why?

EVELYN
He knew how intrigued I was about the one I found in mom's stuff. He was looking for a birthday present, something special. But Wikipedia said you had just the one book of poems ... and nothing was there about your death.

LOLA-80
I have no idea what you're talking about. Wiki--?

EVELYN
Wikipedia. It's online, a kind of group encyclopedia.

LOLA-80
You mean on a computer?

EVELYN
Yes, of course.

LOLA-80
I don't like computers. I still have the Remington I bought used in San Francisco in 1971. Not that I use it very often. It's getting painful to type. It's hard to find ribbons.

EVELYN
It must be an antique.

LOLA-80
I've kept it longer than any of my lovers. Of either sex.

EVELYN
Grandma-- ...

She stops.

LOLA-80
Never censor yourself.

EVELYN
You don't use a computer. You never went to Starbucks until now. You're like Robinson Crusoe. Only a little X-rated.

LOLA-80
X-rated? You should read Lenore Kandel if you want x-rated. Her love poems were banned as obscene. When was that? Nineteen sixty something.

EVELYN
I didn't say--

LOLA-80
--Lenore called her poems holy erotica. Cocks and cunts were part of the cosmic dance.

EVELYN
Grandma--!

LOLA-80
(reciting from memory)
"There are no ways of love but beautiful / I love you all of them / I love you / your cock in my hand / stirs like a bird in my fingers / as you swell and grow hard in my hand--"

EVELYN
Grandma, not so loud ...

LOLA-8
(whispering)
Lenore called this the God/Love poem. They arrested her for it.

EVELYN
I didn't mean you had to whisper.

LOLA-80
She died a few years ago. Wonderful lady. Very smart. Very sensitive.

EVELYN
Was she a friend of yours?

LOLA-80
Only casually. Lenore never compromised. Her poems told the truth. I always looked up to her. She turned down comfort to follow her vision.

EVELYN
She sounds fascinating.

A silence.

LOLA-8O
Do you have a credit card?

EVELYN
Yes, of course.

LOLA-80
I've never had a credit card.

EVELYN
Why do you ask?

LOLA-80
I'm sorry I mentioned it.

EVELYN
Grandma, what are we talking about?

LOLA-80
Nothing really. I never realized credit cards had become such

a big deal. Where were we?

>   EVELYN
> You were telling me about an x-rated poet.

>   LOLA-80
> Only the censors thought of her that way.

Silence.

>   EVELYN
> What was it like to be a beatnik?

>   LOLA-80
> I hate that term.

>   EVELYN
> That's what everybody called you. The beatnik of the family.

>   LOLA-80
> I wasn't interested in becoming a housewife.

In the coffeehouse. Lola-30 at the podium, reading a poem. 1960s.

>   LOLA-30
> America, here are your divorce papers / I can't live with you any more / We are too different // You get noisier every year / with your ad campaigns / with your patriotic speeches / and I cherish silence / for reflection and self-discovery // You think change is progress / and I think change also kills what does not need changing / rituals and cycles lost forever // You are forever buying things / a hoarder of possessions / and my mantra is Less Is More / my essentials on my back // You worship the dollar / and I worship the blade of grass / breaking through the sidewalk // You want to save the world / and I want to save myself // America, here are your divorce papers / I don't want your City on a Hill / I don't want your Manifest

Destiny / I sing the music of the universe / My soul is dancing to Mulligan and Miles / and my spirit soars like a bird

Continuing at Starbucks.

          EVELYN
There's an inscription in mom's book. I assume Grandpa Frank wrote it. I can remember it almost word for word. "This is a book of poems by your mother. She was a very good poet. Unfortunately the world is not kind to poets and she left us too early."

          LOLA-80
I didn't leave my daughter. Frank took her away from me. He thought I was dangerous. I'd raise her to be a free spirit.

          EVELYN
That's funny. I can remember fights when I was young when mom would scream at dad, Watch out! I have a trickle of free spirit in my veins!

          LOLA-80
Good for her.

          EVELYN
But she wasn't a free spirit. She was addicted to all the drugs the doctors gave her. Dad kept the family together. He's a rock.

          LOLA-80
Did you tell me she died?

          EVELYN
Of a heart attack. Shortly after her latest try at treatment. She was in and out most of her life. I swear, my top priority is to keep my children off drugs.

LOLA-80
You have children?

EVELYN
Not yet.

LOLA-80
Are you pregnant?

EVELYN
No, thank God. I'm not ready.

LOLA-80
Why do I think you're married? Did I meet your husband?

EVELYN
You talked to Paul on the phone.

LOLA-80
Really? My memory isn't what it used to be.

EVELYN
What does your doctor say about that?

LOLA-80
Not much. Tell me about your husband.

EVELYN
My fiancée, and I'm not pregnant.

LOLA-80
No woman who isn't pregnant should even be thinking about marriage.

EVELYN
Paul and I love each other.

LOLA-80

Love has nothing to do with it. Marriage exists for children, to give them parents. Otherwise just live together. But no pregnancy, no marriage license. I'd pass a law.

EVELYN

Well, that's a unique way of looking at it.

LOLA-80

It's a very old idea. Bertrand Russell wrote a book about it over 100 years ago. Put "Marriage & Morals" on your reading list. Do young people still read?

EVELYN

Of course I read. The book sounds interesting

LOLA-80

So what do you do, other than avoiding pregnancy?

EVELYN

I'm between jobs actually. My last one was in advertising.

LOLA-80

Lying for a living.

EVELYN

I never looked at it that way.

LOLA-80

You persuade people to buy what they don't need.

EVELYN

It was a job. The agency's been in Grandpa Frank's family for generations.

LOLA-80

Frank was a good artist before he sold out. Is he still alive?

EVELYN
He passed away quite a while ago.

LOLA-80
He used to draw me nude.

EVELYN
No way.

LOLA-80
Are you calling me a liar?

EVELYN
No, I just meant--

LOLA-80
I can remember those days like they were yesterday. If you want to argue about it--

EVELYN
I didn't come here to argue with you.

LOLA-80
What did you come here for?

EVELYN
To meet my grandmother. Why did you agree to see me?

LOLA-80
I did?

EVELYN
Finally, on the phone. You kept changing your mind.

LOLA-80
I don't remember why. I think I had a favor to ask.

EVELYN
What?

LOLA-80
I can't remember.

EVELYN
Maybe you were in shock to learn you had a granddaughter.

LOLA-80
Well, I was certainly surprised.

EVELYN
Me, too, after thinking you were dead for so long. But I knew I had to meet you.

LOLA-80
You deserve to know where you come from.

EVELYN
I'm curious about you, too. Especially after reading your poems.

LOLA-80
What poems?

EVELYN
In your book. Mom had a copy.

LOLA-80
Did you tell me that?

EVELYN
Yes.

LOLA-80
I'm sorry. Sometimes I don't remember things.

EVELYN
Nothing to apologize for.

Silence.

EVELYN
So what do you do to keep busy?

LOLA-80
Why would I want to keep busy?

EVELYN
I was just curious how you spend your day.

LOLA-80
I take a dump first thing in the morning.

EVELYN
Grandma ...

LOLA-80
Then I meditate. I read. I go to a lovely park near my apartment. I read and meditate some more.

EVELYN
Do you have friends?

LOLA-80
I've been blessed with many wonderful friends. I outlived them.

EVELYN
Have you made new ones?

LOLA-80
Old friends can't be replaced.

EVELYN
But it's good to have someone in your life.

LOLA-80
I have my memories.

EVELYN
That sounds lonely.

LOLA-80
Oh no, they're wonderful memories. I'm blessed to have them.

EVELYN
As long as you're happy.

LOLA-80
As long as I keep to myself. All this madness can be catching. The only immunity is isolation.

EVELYN
And the madness is ...?

LOLA-80
Everything! Look around you. Buy this, buy that! Let's have a sale! You don't agree with America? Let's have a war! It gets harder to hide and mind your own business every year.

EVELYN
You're one of a kind, Grandma.

LOLA-80
So are you.

EVELYN
I don't feel like it. I think I have too much time on my hands. I need to get a job.

LOLA-80
What kind of job?

EVELYN
Good question. I'm still trying to figure out what I want to be when I grow up.

LOLA-80
Who says you have to grow up?

Silence.

EVELYN
You were going to tell me where I come from.

LOLA-80
What would you like to know?

EVELYN
How did you meet Grandpa Frank?

In the coffeehouse, Frank is at the podium, 1950s, as scene continues back and forth.

LOLA-80
I met your grandfather at the Genesis Angels Coffeehouse. We were in college and both read poems at the same open mic ...

FRANK
(his poem)
Fuck! Gray! Flannel! / Fuck! Brown! Briefcases! / Fuck! the Water coolers! of America!

LOLA-80
I'd seen him on campus a few times. He reminded me of James Dean.

EVELYN
Love at first sight?

LOLA-80
More like lust at first sight.

EVELYN
Are you kidding me? In the 1950s?

LOLA-80
The fifties were the most radical and liberating years of my life.

EVELYN
Not more so than the sixties.

LOLA-80
The sixties started in the fifties, but then the hippies went on to popularize and pervert the energy. I knew a few people who sold out and became hippies. Most of us hated the attention. We were creating new values, new ways of living. They weren't for everyone, and that was fine. We were ignored, so we didn't have to make compromises. There weren't many of us, and we were underground. Coffeehouses like Genesis Angels let us find one another.

EVELYN
And that's where you met grandpa Frank.

Lola-20 and Frank at a table. Frank is sketching Lola.
Others in the coffeehouse are cardboard figures. Or not there at all.

LOLA-80
He was a better artist than a poet. He came from a wealthy family. It perverted his sense of reality. We were doomed from the beginning.

Frank gives Lola the drawing.

LOLA-20
I'm naked.

FRANK
Wishful thinking.

LOLA-20
I don't look anything like that. My breasts are smaller.

FRANK
Educated guess. Sorry.

LOLA-20
I love my breasts.

FRANK
Did the best I could under the circumstances.

LOLA-20
It's not as if you asked.

FRANK
Meaning ...?

LOLA-20
Is that a question?

FRANK
My pad's only a few blocks away.

LOLA-20
That's convenient.

FRANK
Want to see it?

LOLA-20
Will you draw me nude?

FRANK
If you like.

LOLA-20
I would like.

FRANK
Cool.

EVELYN
Is this the night mom was conceived?

LOLA-80
Heavens no. That comes much later. I moved in with Frank after we graduated and we lived together for several years before everything fell apart. Did I already tell you this?

EVELYN
Grandma, we just met. How did everything fall apart?

LOLA-80
It was the early sixties, and the whole world was beginning to fall apart. Frank came from generations of money but was the family black sheep. He was living on an allowance from his mother. She wanted Frank to go to art school. But we were just hanging out, writing, drawing, doing some traveling ... it felt like paradise for the first year or so.

EVELYN
What happened?

LOLA-80
His dad wanted him to get an MBA and join the family ad agency. There was a lot of pressure on him. Then I got pregnant.

In the coffeehouse.

FRANK
This is not a problem. My sister got knocked up last year. A few days in Mexico, and it's taken care of. She said it was like going to a first class hotel.

LOLA-20
Isn't it expensive?

FRANK
I'll take care of it. Okay?

No reply.

FRANK
Lola, okay?

LOLA-20
Okay.

In Starbucks.

EVELYN
But you didn't go through with it.

LOLA-80
I went to Mexico and chickened out.

EVELYN
How did he take it?

LOLA-80
I never told him. I phoned and planned to. But before I had a chance, he had news of his own. He'd been accepted at Harvard Business School. I couldn't believe it. I told him to go fuck himself and hung up.

EVELYN
This was in Mexico?

LOLA-80
Yes.

EVELYN
Was mom born in Mexico?

LOLA-80
Almost. I stayed for a few months in Ajijic, where there was a large colony of American writers and artists. I loved it there. But my parents tracked me down and convinced me to come home. Angel was born in San Francisco.

EVELYN
When did grandpa Frank find out?

LOLA-80
Not for several years. Then he took Angel away from me. The court gave him sole custody.

EVELYN
What happened?

LOLA-80
He found me at a very bad time. We were living in a car. I was

doing a lot of drugs. Money was tight.

>   EVELYN
>   Were you writing?

>   LOLA-80
>   I was always writing.

>   EVELYN
>   Why didn't you publish more books?

>   LOLA-80
>   I was more interested in doing readings. I liked to see the reaction of the audience.

>   EVELYN
>   Did you try to get joint custody?

>   LOLA-80
>   Of course. The judge said I was a bad mother.

In the coffeehouse. Lola-30 and Frank. Late 1960s. Frank dapper in suit, Lola scruffy.

>   FRANK
>   When you get your act together, we'll talk about visitation rights.

>   LOLA-30
>   Why are you doing this to us?

>   FRANK
>   Look in the mirror, Lola. You're a goddamn mess.

>   LOLA-30
>   At least I didn't sell out.

FRANK
What I did is grow up. It's time for you to do the same.

LOLA-30
What happened to "fuck the water coolers of America"?

FRANK
Go through a treatment program. Then maybe we can talk about Angel.

LOLA-30
I've never been more together.

FRANK
Bullshit. You've never been more strung out. The way you're using, you wouldn't live to see her in high school.

In Starbucks.

LOLA-80
He had a point.

EVELYN
Tell me.

LOLA-80
My demon lover was cocaine. When I got clean the first time, I wanted to arrange time with Angel but Frank had disappeared. I knew he was keeping her from me.

EVELYN
I knew nothing about any of this.

LOLA-80
How could you?

EVELYN
How did you finally get clean for good?

LOLA-80
I got older. Too many of my friends overdosed. Rehab worked when I quit everything.

EVELYN
Wikipedia said you were an English teacher.

LOLA-80
I went back to school and got a teaching job. Good thing, too. It gives me the little Social Security I live on. I'd be homeless again without it.

EVELYN
Grandma, if you need some help--

LOLA-80
I don't. Under the circumstances, I get along just fine.

EVELYN
If you ever need anything--

LOLA-80
I have very few needs. My day is as slow and silent and peaceful as I can make it.

EVELYN
But if something comes up, you have an emergency--

LOLA-80
You're very wealthy. I get the picture.

EVELYN
I won't apologize for being comfortable.

LOLA-80
Is that what you call it?

EVELYN
Why are you attacking me?

LOLA-80
Is that what I'm doing?

EVELYN
Fine. Don't let me help you.

Silence.

LOLA-80
I made you angry.

EVELYN
You have your values, I have mine.

LOLA-80
Very true.

EVELYN
Pardon me if I'm not who you expected.

LOLA-80
I didn't expect anything. Actually you impress me.

EVELYN
How can I possibly impress you?

LOLA-80
You impress me as being a little lost.

EVELYN
What's impressive about that?

LOLA-80
If you're lost, you haven't sold out.

EVELYN
Well, any day now ...

LOLA-80
Maybe. Maybe not. There's no rush, one way or the other.

EVELYN
I don't even know what you mean by selling out.

LOLA-80
Doing whatever is easiest without thinking about it. Living your life out of habit. I can't tell you if you are. Only you can do that.

EVELYN
They're right. You dance to a different drummer.

LOLA-80
I just listen to myself. But it's not easy with all the noisy distractions.

Silence.

EVELYN
I'm glad we met.

LOLA-80
I'm glad we met, too. It's ... Evelyn?

EVELYN
Yes.

LOLA-80
My mind is going.

EVELYN
You seem okay most of the time. When's the last time you saw your doctor?

LOLA-80
Not long ago.

EVELYN
And he said ...

LOLA-80
I'm fine for an old relic from the past.

EVELYN
Good. Grandma, I'm serious about being here for you if you need help.

LOLA-80
Thank you.

Silence.

LOLA-80
There is something.

EVELYN
What?

LOLA-80
I need to rent a car. Apparently you need a credit card. Would you do that for me?

EVELYN
When do you need it?

LOLA-80
As soon as possible. Tomorrow.

EVELYN
I assume you have a driver's license.

LOLA-80
Of course. And never got a ticket.

EVELYN
How long do you need it for?

LOLA-80
Just the day. I have the money.

EVELYN
Yes, I can do that. I can drive if you like.

LOLA-80
I'm doing a day trip with friends.

EVELYN
Then you do have friends.

LOLA-80
Of course I have friends.

EVELYN
I'm sorry. I must have misunderstood you before. We'll rent a car tomorrow morning then.

In the coffeehouse. Lola-40 at the podium. 1972.

LOLA-40

Welcome to Show & Tell Night at Genesis Angels. I want to begin by reading from a manifesto by Lenore Kandel. She wrote this four or five years ago. It was never published but circulated in manuscript among her many friends and admirers.

Lenore Kandel: "Poetry is never compromise. It is the manifestation/translation of a vision, an illumination, an experience. If you compromise your vision, you become a blind prophet."

In Starbucks. Evelyn and Paul at the table.

    PAUL
You've got to be kidding.

    EVELYN
Paul, don't make a mountain out of a molehill.

    PAUL
I can't possibly stay over.

    EVELYN
I'm not asking you to. I'll rent the car tomorrow, return it the next day, and fly home that night. Two days.

    PAUL
How old is she?

    EVELYN
Eighty something.

    PAUL
And she has a license? She can drive?

    EVELYN
Never had a ticket. And she'll be with friends.

He thinks about it.

> PAUL
> So I'll see you in two days.

> EVELYN
> Thank you. I love you.

Continuing in the coffeehouse.

> LOLA-40
> "Two poems of mine, published as a small book, deal with physical love and the invocation, recognition, and acceptance of the divinity in man through the medium of physical love. In other words, it feels so good that you can step outside your private ego and share the grace of the universe. This simple and rather self-evident statement, enlarged and exampled poetically, raised a furor difficult to believe."

Starbucks. Two days later. Evelyn at table, on phone.

> EVELYN
> Paul, I hope you get this before you head to the airport. Grandma never returned the car. I have no idea where she is or what's going on. I'm worried about her. I canceled my flight. I'll call you at home tonight. Hopefully I'll know more.

Continuing in the coffeehouse.

> LOLA-40
> "When a society becomes afraid of its poets, it is afraid of itself. A society afraid of itself stands as another definition of hell."

Starbucks. A few days later. Paul and Evelyn by the table, embraced. They sit.

PAUL
Unbelievable.

EVELYN
I feel so guilty.

PAUL
It wasn't your fault.

EVELYN
I should've demanded to see her license. She didn't even have one. No friends with her either.

PAUL
Don't beat yourself up. She was a demented old lady.

EVELYN
I don't think so. She carefully planned it. She even had the poem on the seat beside her.

PAUL
You mentioned that on the phone. A poem instead of a note. I couldn't follow.

EVELYN
She told me how much she admired this poem and the circumstances of the poet writing it. It all struck me as pretty weird at the time -- but maybe it was a clue about what she was thinking. And I missed it.

PAUL
This guy climbs a mountain and takes off his clothes ...?

EVELYN
... and shoots himself. It's an offering to the buzzards so he can be reborn as a bird. By entering the food chain, he becomes

immortal.

PAUL
Looney tunes.

Continuing in the coffeehouse.

LOLA-40
We lost Lew Welch last year. This is the ending of his last poem, the remarkable "Song of the Turkey Buzzard."
"Hear my Last Will and Testament: / Among my friends there shall always be / one with proper instructions for my continuance. / Let no one grieve. I shall have used it all up / used up every bit of it. / What an extravagance! What a relief!"

Continuing in Starbucks.

EVELYN
She said she wouldn't have the courage to kill herself that way. A cosmic death, she called it. But she certainly got creative, I'll give her that.

PAUL
Not that creative. It was almost an epidemic in Japan some years back. They called it Suicide By Hibachi.

EVELYN
And I rented her the small space she needed to pull it off.

PAUL
Evey, there's no way you could have known what she was up to.

Continuing in coffeehouse.

LOLA-40

"On a marked rock, following his orders, place my meat. / All care must be taken not to frighten the natives of this barbarous land, / who will not let us die, even, as we wish."

Continuing in Starbucks.

PAUL

You don't have to do this.

EVELYN

I want to. She has no one else.

PAUL

How much time will you need?

EVELYN

A few days, I guess. She owns almost nothing. Lots of writing, which I'll save. She mentioned a park where she liked to read and meditate. I'll spread her ashes there.

PAUL

I need you home by next Saturday. There's a company dinner for a new client.

EVELYN

Shouldn't be a problem.

PAUL

Good. I took the liberty of making you a reservation for Wednesday. Give you a couple days to get back to normal. I want you at your sparking best Saturday night. I need to impress this guy.

Continuing in the coffeehouse.

LOLA-40

"With proper ceremony, disembowel what I no longer need, / that it might more quickly rot and tempt my new form / NOT THE BRONZE CASKET BUT THE BRAZEN WING / SOARING FOREVER ABOVE THEE O PERFECT, O SWEETEST WATER / O GLORIOUS WHEELING BIRD"
Lew Welch.

Starbucks. Two days later. Evelyn on the phone.

EVELYN

Paul, it's me. I'm not coming home for a while. I'll be staying with a girlfriend from college. I'm not giving you the number because I don't want you trying to talk me into coming home before I'm ready. This is not about you, and I do love you. This is not about us. This is about me. I've been living my life on automatic pilot, and it's time to stop. I need to find my bearings. I don't know how else to explain it. … I hope your dinner with the client goes well. I'll be in touch. I love you.

She hangs up. She dials another number.

EVELYN

I need to cancel a reservation.

BLACKOUT. The play is over.

FAMILY CLIMATE

TIME: The present and near future

PLACE: Portland, Oregon

CAST:
ANGELA HART, 40s, a widow, homemaker
JOEY HART, her son, a high school senior, bright, idealistic
BRIAN HART, 40s, her brother, a surgeon
HANK HART, 30s, her brother, an art teacher and painter
HOLLY HART, 30s, her sister, a struggling actress
HALLOWEEN CHIEF, an old man in Halloween costume of Indian Chief
AUDIO ELEMENTS: radio broadcasts; voices of historic Indians

SETTING: The entire action takes place in the living room of Angela's modest house.

FAMILY CLIMATE

The play is performed without intermission.

Scene 1

Darkness.

> AUDIO

14 of the 15 hottest years on record have occurred since 2000, the UN says, as global warming continues unabated. This is The Guardian Radio Network.

Lights up. Living room. Angela leads Brian in.

> BRIAN

When's Holly get in?

> ANGELA

Her plane's delayed. She'll take a cab from the airport.

> BRIAN

Hank?

> ANGELA

He arrived this morning. He's looking for high school buddies.

> BRIAN

Why am I not surprised?

ANGELA
You want a drink? Coffee?

BRIAN
I'm fine. I want more detail about Joey than I got on the phone.

ANGELA
I really don't know more.

BRIAN
He refuses to eat. That's it?

ANGELA
And talk.

BRIAN
Protesting the sale, I assume.

ANGELA
I don't know what else it would be.

BRIAN
You once told me he wasn't into family history.

ANGELA
He hasn't been. Getting him to the cabin was like pulling teeth. And now he doesn't want us to sell the land? It doesn't make sense.

BRIAN
I want to see him.

ANGELA
Good luck with that. Last I checked, his door was locked.

BRIAN
He has a lock on his bedroom?

ANGELA
Padlock.

BRIAN
You let him do that?

ANGELA
How could I stop him?

BRIAN
It's your house. He's still a minor.

ANGELA
Not for long.

BRIAN
For now. Angela, you've never been--

ANGELA
Strict enough. I know, I know.

BRIAN
Does he ever unlock the door?

ANGELA
Oh yes. He comes out. He uses the bathroom. He drinks water. He watched the news once.

Brian just looks at her.

ANGELA
Are you sure you don't want a drink? I'm having one.

BRIAN
What happened to sobriety?

ANGELA
Brian, I'm fine. I haven't had trouble in a long time.

BRIAN
Whatever.

A silence as Angela fixes a drink at a mini-bar.

BRIAN
I need to get a room.

ANGELA
I thought you'd be staying here.

BRIAN
(ignoring this)
How about I take everybody out to Jake's for dinner? Those of us who are eating.

ANGELA
I thought I'd order pizza and--

BRIAN
I don't eat pizza for dinner. Will everybody be here at six?

ANGELA
Hank should be. Holly didn't give a time.

BRIAN
I'll pick everybody up at six.

He leaves. Angela drinks.

Blackout.

Scene 2

Darkness.

VOICE IN DARKNESS: CHIEF SEATTLE
This is Chief Seattle. How can you buy or sell the sky, the warmth of the land? The idea is strange to us. If we do not own the freshness of the air and the sparkle of the water, how can you buy them?

Every part of this earth is sacred to my people. Every shining pine needle, every sandy shore, every mist in the dark woods, every clearing and humming insect is holy in the memory and experience of my people. The sap which courses through the trees carries the memories of the red man.

The rivers are our brothers, they quench our thirst. The rivers carry our canoes, and feed our children. If we sell you our land, you must remember, and teach your children, that the rivers are our brothers and yours, and you must henceforth give the rivers the kindness you would give any brother. This is Chief Seattle.

Lights up. That evening. Angela and Brian.
Brian looks at his watch.

BRIAN
Jesus Christ, Angela.

ANGELA
She said she wouldn't be long.

Hank enters from hallway to bedrooms. He carries a sheet of paper.

HANK
I know why. And it's not about the sale. It's about global warming. A manifesto.

He holds up the paper. Brian scoffs.

BRIAN
Terrific.

HANK
Look at this ...

Hank hands Brian the paper.

ANGELA
Then we have nothing to worry about, right? He got over the other times.

HANK
Did he ever go on a hunger strike before?

ANGELA
No. But he was in that tree almost three days before he came down.

HANK
How long has it been since he ate?

ANGELA
This is the fourth day.

HANK
How long before we have to worry?

BRIAN
(reading)
What garbage.

HANK
Doctor Hart?

ANGELA
(to Hank)
He is drinking water.

BRIAN
He'll quit soon enough. He's being theatrical without substance.

HANK
Hope you're right.
(about the manifesto)
So what do you think?

ANGELA
Let me see.

Brian gives Angela the paper. She starts reading.

BRIAN
It's textbook leftwing rhetoric. Same as before.

HANK
When I heard about the hunger strike -- which surprised the hell out of me -- I thought he was protesting the sale.

ANGELA
That's what Holly thought. We all did.

BRIAN
Speaking of which ... how long do we have to wait for her? I made reservations for seven. I'm not being late, with or without her.

ANGELA
You two go ahead. This is amazing, coming from him. The part about the Pope. I could never drag him to church.

BRIAN
You plan to drive?

ANGELA
I'm fine.

BRIAN
Whatever. I'm going to talk to him.

He exits via the hallway.

HANK
Hasn't changed.

ANGELA
None of us change, Hank. That's this family's cross to bear.

HANK
He does have a point. If you believe the scientists anyway.

ANGELA
You don't believe them?

HANK
I don't know who to believe any more.

ANGELA
It's so unlike him to admire a Pope. You don't think he'd become a Catholic, do you?

HANK
If he does, nobody tell mom. How's she doing?

ANGELA
Worse. She doesn't always know who I am.

HANK
That must be hard to take. I'll visit tomorrow after we sign the papers.

ANGELA
She actually acts more relaxed, more happy, than before. When she recognized me ...

HANK
Mom relaxed? I won't believe that till I see it. Does she know we're selling the property?

ANGELA
She did when Brian got power of attorney. Probably not now.

HANK
Just as well, don't you think?

ANGELA
Absolutely. Do you ever get second thoughts?

HANK
Of course.

ANGELA
How did Brian change your mind? The money?

Hank smiles.

HANK
If I said the money didn't matter, I'd be lying.

ANGELA
It would buy you lots of time to paint. No more teaching.

HANK
Parking cars.

ANGELA
You're not teaching?

HANK
Between gigs.

ANGELA
Oh Hank ...

HANK
Stop it. To get back to your question, I've always found the whole resort idea distasteful. Ski lodge, condos, golf course ... I don't know people who go to places like that.

ANGELA
You know Brian.

HANK
Exactly.

ANGELA
What changed your mind?

HANK
Holly.

ANGELA
Really?

HANK
You sound surprised.

ANGELA
I never thought of her as the argumentative type.

HANK
She didn't try and convince me. She told me why she changed her mind and would sign.

ANGELA
Why did she?

HANK
It's personal and private. I gave my word.

Angela thinks a moment.

ANGELA
She needs money for an abortion.

Hank shrugs.

ANGELA
I'm right, I can tell. But I don't see what that has to do with your feelings about it.

HANK
If she had a personal emergency--

ANGELA
An abortion.

HANK
Whatever it might be. I can see how a nest egg for emergencies could come in handy.

ANGELA
For the money then.

HANK
Okay, for the money. It makes me sound so unprincipled. But when you live paycheck to paycheck ...

ANGELA
You don't have to convince me. I definitely decided for the money.

Brian returns.

HANK
Any luck?

BRIAN
Doing what?

HANK
Talking to him? Whatever?

BRIAN
I told him the basic facts of Reality 101 through a closed door. I think he's smoking pot in there.

HANK
He wasn't when I saw him.

ANGELA
You actually saw him? He let you in?

HANK
I saw him briefly when he passed out the manifesto.

BRIAN
Look, I'm going to Jake's so I don't lose the reservation. Will you be right behind me or what?

ANGELA
I should wait for Holly.

                    BRIAN
She knows where Jake's is. Leave a note on the door.

The doorbell rings.

                    ANGELA
That must be her.

She exits to answer door.

                    BRIAN
I think you should drive.

                    HANK
Aye aye, captain.

                    BRIAN
Grow up, Hank.

Exits to leave.
Angela and Holly enter.

                    HOLLY
    (To front door)
Nice seeing you, too, Brian!
    (To others)
After two years. Whatever it's been. Since Joe's funeral.

                    HANK
Sis.

                    HOLLY
Bro.

They embrace.

ANGELA
Brian made reservations at Jake's. We'd better get going.

HOLLY
Is Joey coming?

ANGELA
Just us.

HANK
It's a long story.

ANGELA
You must be beat. If you'd rather stay and take a nap ...

HOLLY
And pass up a free dinner at Jake's? You know Brian will pick up the tab.

HANK
But not the bar bill.

HOLLY
Right. Well, better than nothing. I'm ready to go whenever.

HANK
Then let's do it.

ANGELA
(To Hank)
Would you drive?

She gives him the car keys.

Blackout.

Scene 3

Darkness.

> AUDIO
> The future will see a devastating worldwide food crisis, the UN says. Global grain reserves are at critically low levels, and rising food prices threaten disaster and unrest. This is The Guardian Radio Network.

Lights up.
Later that night.
Joey is eating pizza, wearing earphones.
Angela and Hank enter.

> ANGELA
> You're eating! Thank God.

> HANK
> Good to see you back.

> ANGELA
> Joey, you look pale. I think tomorrow you should--

> JOEY
> I'm fine, mom. I'm fantastical. This is becoming so awesome ... the manifesto is just the tip of the iceberg.

> HANK
> You're losing me, Joey.

> JOEY
> I think I've started a revolution. My Twitter followers more than double every day. And on Facebook, GABI has almost ten thousand likes!

ANGELA
Who's Gabby?

JOEY
G - A - B - I. Give America Back to the Indians.

HANK
Oh boy ...

ANGELA
What on earth are you talking about?

HANK
Are you sure they even want it after the mess we made?

JOEY
That's the point. Obviously we can't fix the planet. Everything we try to do, which isn't much, ends up making global warming worse.

ANGELA
GABI is what? A club, a Facebook page?

JOEY
A movement.

HANK
What the hell, why not?

ANGELA
A movement to give the country back to the Indians. You can't be serious, and you have no way of doing it even if you were.

JOEY
It's an attention grabber. Like a metaphor. But we're already developing an awesome plan of action.

HANK
I'd like to hear it.

JOEY
We're still polishing it. Mr. Franks is helping us.

HANK
A teacher?

ANGELA
His controversial history teacher.

JOEY
You think he was controversial before!

HANK
Is GABI your idea or his?

JOEY
I can't remember whose but definitely not his. Ideas were being texted around like crazy. At first the goal was to get our parents' attention with a hunger strike and then present a manifesto and get them involved. Then it was no, we can't depend on adults, we have to do this ourselves. And then we realized only Indians have ever lived in harmony with the Earth. If anybody knew how to fix things, they would. Isn't this an awesome idea?

ANGELA
I'm not amused. You be careful. College entrance people don't like controversy.

JOEY
If we're all dead, what difference does it make?

ANGELA
Don't make this sound like a nuclear war.

JOEY
Hello? It's worse.

ANGELA
If that were true, then the government would--

JOE
The government is dysfunctional. A lot of them deny the problem.

ANGELA
Maybe they have access to secret information that--

JOEY
You have your head in the sand.

ANGELA
That's no way to talk to your mother.

HANK
Time out! Time out!

They calm down.

HANK
There's plenty of time to save the world in the morning. For the moment, I'm beat and I believe this is my bedroom.

ANGELA
I'll get sheets.

She exits.

JOEY
Actually there's not plenty of time. Glaciers have been melting much faster than predicted.

HANK
I get it, Joey. I just don't know what can be done about it.

JOEY
Because Americans can't do anything about it. We have the wrong philosophy. We're capitalists, which feeds on growth.

HANK
So you want the Indians to figure it out.

JOEY
The President declares a national state of emergency. He creates a governing board to create a new policy of redemption and environmental renewal. The board consists of American Indians, preferably descendants of elders. I mean, they lived in harmony with Nature for centuries. They know how to do it. So we put them in charge.

HANK
Asking them to help us may be asking a lot.

JOEY
We have to try. We have to do something.

HANK
You ever hear of Lew Welch?

JOEY
No.

HANK
He's a poet. One of the forgotten Beats. One of his poems ends this way ... I'm paraphrasing: You can't fix it. You can't

make it go away. I don't know what you're going to do about it but I know what I'm going to do about it. I'm just going to walk away from it. Maybe a small part of it will die if I'm not around feeding it anymore.

> JOEY
> That really sucks.

> HANK
> Maybe it's too late to fix it. It's certainly not going away.

> JOEY
> You think we should watch our own extinction without trying to stop it? Why not just commit mass suicide?

> HANK
> I'd rather dance on the Titanic. That's what life amounts to now.

Angela enters with sheets.

> ANGELA
> Who's dancing on the Titanic?

> JOEY
> He thinks everybody should commit mass suicide. I can't believe you'd think that.

He heads for his room.

> HANK
> Actually we'll be colonizing Mars ...
>   (To Angela)
> He's really been giving a lot of thought to this stuff.

> ANGELA
> I wish he wouldn't.

They start making a bed on the divan.

          ANGELA
Obviously the weather's changing ... but how does it follow that the world is coming to an end?

          HANK
Have to ask Joey on that. Not my pay grade.

          ANGELA
Did he say anything about End Times and the Second Coming?

Hank is amused.

          HANK
Relax. That's not where he's coming from.

          ANGELA
Thank God for that.

They continue making the bed.

Blackout.

Scene 4

Darkness.

          AUDIO
In addition to a food shortage, the UN warns that an even greater global crisis will be caused by a shortage of fresh water. As reservoirs dry up across the globe, a billion people will have no access to safe drinking water. Rationing and a battle to control supplies will follow, bringing disaster and unrest. This is

The Guardian Radio Network.

> VOICE IN DARKNESS: OHIYESA
>
> This is Ohiyesa. It was our belief that the love of possessions is a weakness to be overcome. Its appeal is to the material part, and if allowed its way, it will in time disturb one's spiritual balance. Therefore, children must early on learn the beauty of generosity. They are taught to give what they prize most, that they may taste the happiness of giving. This is Ohiyesa.

Lights up.
The next day.
Holly storms in, followed by Angela. Holly is looking for something.

> HOLLY
>
> Where in hell do you keep the booze?

> ANGELA
>
> Whiskey and glasses over there. More variety in the kitchen cabinet. What do you want?

> HOLLY
>
> Anything.

> ANGELA
>
> Bourbon and water?

> HOLLY
>
> Great. A double.

> ANGELA
>
> I'll get ice.

Angela leaves. Brian and Hank have entered.

> BRIAN
>
> Now there's this family's universal cure all: let's have a drink!

HOLLY
Brian, I told you at the lawyer's, I have nothing more to say. I'm following my gut feeling. You can't change my mind.

BRIAN
I don't want to change your mind.

HOLLY
Of course you do. If I don't sign, then there's no deal.

BRIAN
Unless you're no longer in the family corporation.

HOLLY
What do you mean?

BRIAN
You sell your parcel to me and resign. Then what happens has nothing to do with you. You don't have to deal with your dirty developers. And you get money, which I know you can use.

HOLLY
But the land still goes to the developers.

BRIAN
So what? You have nothing to do with it one way or another. You're selling to your brother. Flesh and blood!

HOLLY
Who turns around and sells to those bastards!
(Angela brings Holly her drink. She has one for herself.)

Brian looks at his watch, making sure Angela notices.

HANK
Holly, you need to consider this. It does let us off the hook.

HOLLY
He's buying you out, too?

HANK
Look at it this way. You sell your car to someone. They go out and run over and kill a bicyclist. Should you be arrested for murder?

HOLLY
No way.

HANK
Exactly. This is no different. We're selling to Brian. What he does after that is his business. If bad karma results, it's his problem, not ours.

ANGELA
Hank, can I get you a drink?

BRIAN
Angela--

HANK
Nothing, thanks.

ANGELA
A glass of milk, Brian?

BRIAN
(Ignoring this)
I need an answer before four. I'm still flying home tonight.

HANK
It's the best deal we're going to get.

> HOLLY
I'll think about it.

> BRIAN
I'll call here at three to get your answer. Try not to get too polluted.

> HANK
We were going to visit mom after signing. She'd like to see us all together.

> ANGELA
I don't think she'll recognize us.

> HOLLY
I can't handle that.

> BRIAN
I'll visit her after lunch. Three, Holly.

He leaves.

> HANK
I'll have that drink now.

Blackout.

Scene 5

Darkness.

> VOICE IN DARKNESS: OHIYESA
This is Ohiyesa. The Wise Man believes profoundly in silence - the sign of a perfect equilibrium. Silence is the absolute poise or balance of body, mind and spirit. The man who preserves his selfhood ever calm and unshaken by the storms of existence -

not a falling leaf, as it were, not a ripple upon the surface of a pool - this man has the ideal attitude and conduct of life. Silence is the cornerstone of character. This is Ohiyesa.

Lights up.
Living room. That afternoon.
Holly is on her cell phone.

          HOLLY
I feel guilty because sis and Hank were probably counting on the money....

Hank enters.

          HOLLY
Honey, I have to run. Love you.

She hangs up.

          HANK
Everything copasetic?

          HOLLY
Bob suggested we keep a few acres around the cabin for ourselves.

          HANK
Didn't we decide against that a few years back?

          HOLLY
I can't remember. I have no head for business.

          HANK
So when Brian calls ...?

          HOLLY
I won't be here. I chickened out and sent him an email. Same

answer. Short and sweet.

>HANK
>I thought you needed the money.

>HOLLY
>My problem took care of itself. For once, the universe was listening to me.

>HANK
>Okay. We'll leave it at that.

>HOLLY
>I'm really sorry if I'm making life harder than you expected.

>HANK
>Don't worry about it. I've gotten very good at going with the flow. Have a safe trip.

They embrace.

>HOLLY
>I love you, mister painter man.

>HANK
>Love you back.

Holly waits for more.

>HOLLY
>Well? Love you back what?

>HANK
>I thought you quit.

>HOLLY
>Bob made me go back. I start rehearsals for "Same Time,

Next Year" when I get home.

>**HANK**
>All right then ... that's a great role.

They embrace again.

>**HANK**
>Love you back, madam theater lady.

>**HOLLY**
>It's just the community theater.

>**HANK**
>Cut the "just" crap. A stage is a stage is a stage.

A long embrace.
Blackout.

Lights up.
A few hours later.

Hank stretched out on the divan, awake.
Joey enters with a back pack, coming from school.

>**HANK**
>Hey, Che ...

>**JOEY**
>Very funny. We're going to be bigger than Che. We'll be as big as Tom Paine. We're writing a new Common Sense.

>**HANK**
>More power to you.

>**JOEY**
>Where's mom?

ANGELA
(Entering)
She's right here. How long did I sleep?

HANK
Couple hours.

ANGELA
I must've been tired.

JOEY
Or feeling guilty about selling the family legacy.

HANK
We didn't sign. Holly backed out.

JOEY
I have the most awesome aunt in the world!

ANGELA
What should I make for dinner?

JOEY
I'm going to Bruce's for pizza.

ANGELA
On a school night?

JOEY
We have a lot of work to do. And Mr. Franks is giving us credit for it.

HANK
For how to give the country back to the Indians?

JOEY
For devising a strategy of transition.

ANGELA
Does the principal know what Mr. Franks is encouraging?

JOEY
Mom, this is really important. I can't believe how fast GABI is growing! There's already over a dozen chapters organized in four states. This idea is so hot!

He exits to bedroom.

ANGELA
Were we like that?

HANK
Sure we were.

ANGELA
Youth has to rebel against something, I suppose.

HANK
Given the way the world is, the world his generation is inheriting, I can understand where their energy is coming from.

ANGELA
I think this whole weather deal is being blown out of proportion. If we can walk on the moon, we can fix the weather.

HANK
But will we?

ANGELA
If it gets bad enough, of course we will. This country isn't about ignoring problems. Sometimes we're slow, but we always get it done.

HANK
A lady of faith.

ANGELA
Of course I have faith.

Joey comes in, passing on his way out.

JOEY
You have faith in myths, mom.

ANGELA
Don't stay out late. It's a school night. That boy.

HANK
Actually I'm impressed with how serious he is - even about the dumbest idea I've ever heard.

ANGELA
I don't know about teachers today. They seem to encourage that sort of thing. Are you ready for a drink?

HANK
In a bit. I want to talk to you about something.

ANGELA
If it's about the land--

HANK
It isn't. I'm moving here. I got a job at the community college.

ANGELA
What? When?

HANK
A few weeks ago. I didn't want to bring it up while we were

dealing with the sale.

ANGELA
I thought Jane loved it there.

HANK
We broke up. It's not something I want to get into. She found someone with more financial stability than an artist. An accountant.

ANGELA
Hank, I'm so sorry.

HANK
No sooner did that happen than I was denied tenure. So the last few months have been a mad, stressful scramble of sending out resumes. I got three interviews and two offers. I chose here.

ANGELA
That's wonderful. I mean--

HANK
I know what you mean.

ANGELA
Have you found a place to stay?

HANK
That's what I wanted to talk to you about. I want to rent your basement.

ANGEL
To live in?

HANK
Exactly.

ANGELA
Have you been down there lately?

HANK
Let's go right now. It can't be worse than some of the hovels I've lived in.

ANGELA
Don't decide until you see it.

HANK
And don't you under-estimate my decorative talent after spending a few hours at Goodwill. I can sleep there, work there ... bring my female students there ...

Angela playfully jabs him as they head out.

Blackout.

Scene 6

Darkness.

AUDIO
In the near future, victims of climate change will make the West pay for their losses and suffering. The scientific case is strengthening that developed countries are to blame for global warming and the disasters that result. There soon will be a legal reckoning, say lawyers representing the victims. This is The Guardian Radio Network.

Lights up.
A few days later.
Joey is showing Angela how to take a video on his iPhone.

JOEY
And press the button here. The main thing is make sure I'm in frame. Just don't freak out. It's really easy.

ANGELA
For your generation, I'm sure ...
(Joey moves a few feet away and faces the camera. Angela makes an effort.)

During this, Hank comes up from the basement.

ANGELA
I don't see you ...

JOEY
Mom!

HANK
Let me.

He takes the camera.

JOEY
It's a video.

HANK
Going first class.

JOEY
For recruitment on my Facebook page.

HANK
Let's do it.
    (Playing the part)
Places! Quiet on the set! Action!

JOEY

This is Joey. I'm a senior at Roosevelt High and the founder, one of the founders, of GABI. I'm about to leave for school on the day of our first walkout protest. At exactly 10:15 this morning, west coast time, I'll be with at least 50 students from my school to leave classes in protest of the government's failure to address global warming in any serious way. We will march to City Hall for a political rally and won't return to classes until after lunch. We are not the only school doing this. So far, almost one hundred high schools in twenty three states will have students leaving classes at exactly 10:15 Pacific time. We chose this time because it's the approximate time of death of Sitting Bull after being murdered on the reservation in North Dakota. GABI, or Give America Back to the Indians, is growing faster than any of us thought possible in our wildest dreams. If you are a high school student and want to save the planet and save the extinction of the human race, please join us. Remember, don't trust anyone over twenty!

A silence.

JOEY

Cut!

HANK

What's this over twenty stuff? What about the teacher who's helping you?

JOEY

We don't work with him any more. He didn't want us to do this.

ANGELA

You never told me that.

JOEY

There's lots I don't tell you. I'm running late. Thanks,

Uncle Hank.

HANK
Be safe.

Joey leaves.

ANGELA
Tell me I shouldn't be worried.

HANK
They have to feel like they're not powerless. I remember how I felt when we invaded Iraq. In my gut it felt like a great mistake, and I had to express myself. Marching in protest seemed the only way.

ANGELA
What if he gets arrested? It'll be on his record when he applies for college. At the very least, it would make him less likely for a scholarship.

HANK
I don't think anyone is getting arrested.

ANGELA
You're always so optimistic.

HANK
Not really. But I wish it were true.

Blackout.

Scene 7

Darkness.

VOICE IN DARKNESS: CROWFOOT

This is Crowfoot. What is life? It is the flash of a firefly in the night. It is the breath of a buffalo in the wintertime. It is the little shadow which runs across the grass and loses itself in the sunset.

Our land is more valuable than your money. It will last forever. It will not even perish by the flames of fire. This is Crowfoot.

Lights up.
A month later.
Hank is shooting video of Joey.

JOEY

This is Joey. Last night, when I checked Facebook a little after midnight, I learned that GABI registered its one hundred thousandth member. And last week we added our one hundredth high school. But I have even better news. Last week, on the Pine Ridge Reservation, students formed NAIM, the New American Indian Movement, and they will partner with GABI to bring our first Indians into the revolution for rebirth. This is an important and necessary step toward bringing the descendants of native elders into decision-making positions in a new government. With this coalition, we can aim even higher. How does a two million student march on Washington sound? Stay tuned. And don't trust anyone over twenty.

Hank stops filming.
Blackout.

Lights up.
A few days later.

Angela on the home phone, listening.
Joey starts through the room, on his way out

> ANGELA

Alice, I have to call you back.
She hangs up.
> Just a minute, young man! Get back in here.

> JOEY

Mom, I'm running late.

> ANGELA

Get in here and sit!

Joey does. He's not used to seeing her this angry.

> ANGELA

This has got to stop.

> JOEY

I can't stop. I've got two hundred thousand kids counting on me.

> ANGELA

I'm not talking about politics. I'm talking about how your grades are slipping. A "B" in computer science? You've always had A's.

> JOEY

I'm getting punished for GABI. The teacher's a Republican.

> ANGELA

That's no excuse.

> JOEY

It's no big deal. I'll do an extra credit project.

ANGELA
I think it's a very big deal. And to show you how serious I am, you're grounded for the weekend.

JOEY
You can't ground me.

ANGELA
I'm your mother. I can do anything I want.

JOEY
What if I ignore you?

ANGELA
I'll call the police, they'll call Social Services, and eventually you'll be put in a foster home. Then see how much freedom you have.

JOEY
That's totally absurd.

ANGELA
Try me.

He's never seen her like this.

You'll thank me soon enough when you apply for college.

JOEY
You have your head in the sand! How can I apply for college if there isn't a planet left to live on?

He exits to his room.
Angela breathes deeply, trying to calm down.
Blackout

Lights up. That night.
Angela and Hank. Angela is agitated.

ANGELA
He's never done something like this before. I'm calling the police.

HANK
Sis, it's obvious where he went. There's a rally and powwow in the park.

ANGELA
A powwow?

HANK
Indians are getting more involved with what the kids started. A bunch of Chiefs will be leading the march in Washington.

ANGELA
He certainly won't be marching in that one.

HANK
You've got to let him go.

ANGELA
You're taking his side on this?

HANK
No. He needs to be punished but stopping him from participating in history is not the way to do it.

ANGELA
History, shmistory ...

HANK
It may prove to be important history, if they can actually get more than a million kids out there. And Joey's at the ground

floor of all this. Your Joey. My nephew. I'm still pinching myself. If you take this away from him, he'll never forgive you for it.

She thinks about it.

> HANK
> Let me talk to him. He made an error in priorities. I'll tell him he can go on the march in Washington if he stays grounded until then and catches up on his schoolwork.

> ANGELA
> Improves his grades.

> HANK
> Improves his grades. What do you say?

> ANGELA
> I'll tell him tonight.

> HANK
> No. You go to bed. I'll wait up and talk to him.

> ANGELA
> You really like Joey.

> HANK
> Yes, I do.

> ANGELA
> You don't think he's ruining his life?

> HANK
> No, I don't.

> ANGELA
> Very well. Goodnight then.

          HANK
   Night, sis.

She exits.
Blackout.

Lights up half.
Later, almost midnight.

Hank dozes in a chair.
The front door opens. Joey enters, heading for his room.

          HANK
   We need to talk.

Joey jumps.

          JOEY
   You scared me.

          HANK
   You're scaring your mother. Sit down.

          JOEY
   She has--

          HANK
   --her head in the sand, I know. Sit.
      (Joey will.)
   I'm inclined to agree with you. But she's still your mother. She worries like hell about you because she loves you so much.

          JOEY
   She's out of touch, Uncle Hank. She keeps bringing up my college application.

HANK
She gets to make the rules in this house, Joey. You did a really dumb thing tonight.

JOEY
GABI was invited to the powwow and--

HANK
--and you got to feel like a big shot. You got a lot of recognition, am I right?

JOEY
They did a special drumming in our honor. It was so awesome.

HANK
Listen to yourself. What does being a big shot have to do with getting government action on climate change? I'll tell you what. Not a goddamn thing. It's frosting on the cake, and if it tastes too good, you're going to lose your focus. On the other hand, if you get a million high school kids marching on Washington--

JOEY
--much more than a million.

HANK
This has the potential to really change history. Why would you jeopardize this moment for a taste of frosting? Because your mother was going to forbid you going to Washington. And she has the power to do it.

JOEY
If she gives me to a foster family--

HANK
Dammit, Joey, don't make this so complicated. I talked to her

on your behalf. If you stay grounded until the march, and get your grades back up where they belong, you can go to Washington.

JOEY
You did that for me? Why?

HANK
You remind me a little of myself at your age. Believe it or not, I've been in protest marches. I've been tear-gassed. I even spent a night in jail.

JOEY
What were you protesting?

HANK
The Iraq war. The second one. Regime change with shock and awe. We got gassed, some of us got arrested, and my parents decided to teach me a lesson by refusing to bail me out.

JOEY
So did it work?

HANK
Of course not. But I did get more careful. Which is exactly what you should do. Progressive struggles take a lot if time.

A silence.

HANK
I'm ready for bed.

JOEY
Thanks for dealing with mom.

HANK
No problem. You're blowing my mind actually. A million kids

will be a sight to see.

> JOEY
> Two million.

> HANK
> There are what, twenty million high school students in the country? Ten percent is a big order.

> JOEY
> But we're all on the same planet. The next step is going international.

> HANK
> Get the hell to bed before I become an idealist again. And remember, you can't trust me. I'm over twenty.

Blackout.

Scene 8

Darkness.

> AUDIO
> On April 25, 2004, over one million marchers gathered on the National Mall in support of women's reproductive rights, making it "the largest protest in U.S. history," according to march organizers. News media estimated the crowd at under a million, closer to the Million Man March of 1995. Today those marches were made small by almost two million high school students who call themselves GABI, Give America Back to the Indians. And the New American Indian Movement, also led by high school students, seems to agree, taking their place at the front of the parade. How exactly the country could be given back to the Indians has never been made clear to this reporter. This is the Guardian Radio Network.

Lights up.
Late afternoon, after the march.
Angela on the home phone.

          ANGELA
That's wonderful, Joey...
Hank has entered.
   Your Uncle Hank wants to say hi.

She hands him the phone.

          HANK
You must be walking on air....We're both proud of you.

          ANGELA
Tell him to get to bed early so he doesn't miss his plane in the morning.

          HANK
Your mother doesn't want you to stay out late. You have an early flight....Really? What's her name?....Have fun, Joey. You deserve it.

He hangs up.

          ANGELA
What do you mean, have fun? Whose name?

          HANK
There's a party. He met a girl named Amanda.

          ANGELA
A party with drinking, I suppose. You know where that leads.

          HANK
He had an incredible day.

The home phone rings.
    Let him enjoy it.
He answers.
    Hello....We were just talking to him....It went amazingly well.

> ANGELA
> Who is it?

> HANK
> Your sister wants to talk to you.

He hands Angela the phone.

> HANK
> Holly.

> ANGELA
> Hi....I'm a nervous wreck. Joey met a girl.

Blackout.

Lights up.
Hours later.
Angela and Hank look tired, tense.

> ANGELA
> It's only a three hour drive. Why does she stay with him?

> HANK
> I never understood what she saw in any of them. I can't believe I didn't pick up that something was wrong.

> ANGELA
> She's a good actress.

The home phone rings.

            HANK
    Finally.
He picks up.
    Hello....It is. Who is this?...Go to hell yourself, you
sonofabitch.
He hangs up.
    So much for no backlash.

            ANGELA
    Who was it?

            HANK
    Some crank. He doesn't approve of your parenting skills.

Holly enters.

            HOLLY
    I let myself in.

            ANGELA
    (Going to her)
    How are you?

            HOLLY
    A complete wreck, to be honest.

            HANK
    One of these days, you're going to have to--

            HOLLY
    I can't do this tonight. Right now I just want a drink and a hot
bath.

            ANGELA
    In what order?

HOLLY
At the same time.

ANGELA
I'll fill the tub. Hank will make you a drink.

She exits.

HANK
Let me look at you....I was expecting worse.

HOLLY
I've gotten better at ducking.

HANK
I could say something.

HOLLY
You don't have to. This time I'm leaving.

HANK
I hope you mean that.

HOLLY
You know what's ironic? He used to hit me because he thought I was cheating on him. This time it was because I discovered he's been cheating on me. For almost a year.

HANK
Christ.

HOLLY
At least it's the kick in the ass I obviously needed. Now I won't even live in the same town with him.

HANK
You're moving?

HOLLY
I was thinking of coming here. I think it will be good for me to be close to Angela. I always feel better after talking to her. She's my rock.

ANGELA
(Off stage)
Water's ready!

HANK
I'll make that drink.

Blackout.

Lights up half.
After midnight. Holly is in bed on the divan.

The home phone starts ringing. Holly sleepily heads for it.

HOLLY
Hello ...

Angela enters in her robe.

ANGELA
What's wrong?

HOLLY
This is her sister. Just a minute.

She gives Angela the phone.

ANGELA
This is Angela ...

(She gasps.)

          HOLLY
Sis? What is it?

Angela is losing it.
Blackout.

Lights up.
A short time later.

Hank, in a robe, is on the phone.
Holly comforts Angela.

          HANK
All I know is they crashed the party and beat the shit out of everyone. Joey got it worse than most....Brian, does it really matter at this point? What's important is to get her on a plane as soon as possible. If I had the money--....Perfect. You're a life saver.

          HOLLY
I want to talk to him.

          HANK
Holly wants to talk to you.
    (To Angela, handing Holly the phone.)
Get packed.

Angela exits.

          HOLLY
Brian, I'm ready to sign....I am serious....Because a situation like this brings home how useless it is to have wealth you can't even access. Our land feels more like a curse than a legacy....Works for me. Goodnight.

She hangs up.

        HANK
Do you know what you're doing?

        HOLLY
I haven't a clue. But I'm doing it.

Blackout.

Scene 9

Darkness.

        VOICE IN DARKNESS: CRAZY HORSE
This is Crazy Horse. After suffering beyond suffering, the Red Nation shall rise again and it shall be a blessing for a sick world.

I see a time of Seven Generations when all the colors of mankind will gather under the Sacred Tree of Life and the whole Earth will become one circle again. In that day, there will be those among the Lakota who will carry knowledge and understanding of unity among all living things, and the young white ones will come to those of my people and ask for this wisdom. This is Crazy Horse.

        AUDIO
Backlash against the high school organization GABI, Give America Back to the Indians, continues to grow. According to a new CNN poll, seventy one percent of the parents of GABI members are putting new restrictions on their children's participation. And the last of the GABI teenagers hospitalized after a violent attack by the Sons of Satan motorcycle club has been released from the hospital and is on his way home. This is the Guardian News Network.

Lights up.

A few weeks later.
Hank and Holly.

        HOLLY
We should have put the banner in here. Or made two banners.

        HANK
Bedroom's much better. He won't expect it. In here, it's practically a cliché. First, we give him a little disappointment. Where's the grand welcome with balloons, banners and the rest? Then he goes into his bedroom and we hit him with both barrels.

        HOLLY
I think I heard a car door.
A quick exit and return to look
    They're here! What did we decide? Song or no song?

        HANK
No song. We need to play it by ear.

        HOLLY
I'm really nervous.

        HANK
I'm sure he is, too.

        HOLLY
I'll just tell him I love him and he looks great.

        HANK
And if he looks like shit, you'll insult him. By ear, Holly. When in doubt, say nothing.

        HOLLY
I'll say nothing.

Angela, Brian and Joey enter. Joey is on crutches. It's hard for him to walk with them.

HOLLY
Joey!
She rushes to him.
I've been so worried about you. But you look wonderful! I love you so much.

HANK
Welcome home, Joey.

ANGELA
What can I get you?

JOEY
I'm really tired. I'd just like to take a nap. Would that be okay?

ANGELA
Of course you can take a nap.

Joey heads for the bedroom. He notices Angela and Holly are following him.

JOEY
I don't need any help.

ANGELA
I want to make sure your room's in order.

Threesome exit.

BRIAN
Christ, Hank. You could've put up some balloons.

HANK
We did the royal treatment in his bedroom. Listen.

A beat. Then squeals from Angela and Holly. No sound from Joey.

BRIAN
Very nice. I hope you don't have dinner plans because I managed to get everybody together to sign the papers this evening. We meet in the bar at The Hilton at seven.

HANK
We all have to be there?

BRIAN
You have a date? Break it.

HANK
Just curious.

BRIAN
Dad put it in the will, you know that.

HANK
Legalese goes in one ear and out the other.

BRIAN
Which may have something to do with your lack of wealth.

HANK
My lack of wealth follows directly from being an artist in this sex crazy, sports crazy, star worshiping culture I live in.

BRIAN
I seem to recall hearing about a few artists who have done quite well for themselves.

HANK
The stars. There's only room for a few.

BRIAN
If the public doesn't like what you're painting, paint something else.

HANK
Art has nothing to do with satisfying the public.

BRIAN
Not only are you a liberal, if not a radical, but an ivory tower elitist.

HANK
Whatever you say, Brian.

BRIAN
Condescension may work in the university, but it doesn't work with me.

HANK
My humble apologies. I'm going to see if everything is okay.

BRIAN
One more thing while we're alone. I've been wanting to tell you this for some time.

HANK
Shoot.

BRIAN
It's taken me a while but I think I figured out what makes you leftwing types tick. You're romantics. Some in the closet, some not, but you look at the world as if it's some kind of Eden. Forget all the snakes and deception and betrayal, it's your version of paradise. Whenever you talk about Nature, it's all snow-capped mountains and bubbling brooks. About Indians, it's peace on earth, no matter tribes were fighting each other then with all the ferocity of tribes in the Middle East today. You focus

on a small corner of Nature and forget the rest. You leave out the lion stalking, killing, eating a deer. You leave out the buzzard ripping out the organs of only half-dead prey. In Nature, the real natural world, killing and violence are everywhere. You even find it at home. You ever watch a cat torture a mouse? Fun and games for the cat, but damn unpleasant for Mickey. You say it's a crime to torture terrorists but this behavior didn't come out of thin air. It's natural. It's in the DNA of animal life itself. And we're all animals, Hank, no matter how often we deny it. Ever hear the expression "Nature red in tooth and claw"?

    HANK

Tennyson.

    BRIAN

So you know the reality. You just don't believe it. Is that it?

    HANK

There's a lot more to it than that.

    BRIAN

Just as there's more to all those kids on the street. GABI isn't a protest, it's a party. You ever look closely at their faces on television? They're having a ball! It's just like the sixties: here today, gone tomorrow. As the kids understand how dangerous it is out there, they'll go back to video games. GABI is history.

    HANK

And I thought I was the cynic of the family.

    BRIAN

Well, I got it said. Tell Angela I need to talk to her before I go.

    HANK

I'll do that.

He exits.

Brian regards the room with its Goodwill decor. He obviously finds it distasteful.

Angela enters.

> ANGELA
> You wanted to see me?

> BRIAN
> I decided to stay over a day or two to make sure you get situated.

> ANGELA
> Situated how?

> BRIAN
> So you're safe, like we talked about. Getting a hand gun, taking a safety class.

> ANGELA
> But I didn't say yes.

> BRIAN
> Don't you watch the news? Vigilantes are targeting homes where GABI members live. You have to protect yourself.

> ANGELA
> We did get a few crank calls. And a sign was put on the lawn when I was at the hospital. Hank took care of it.

> BRIAN
> What did the sign say?

> ANGELA
> Bad parents raise bad kids.

BRIAN
I'd fault a certain uncle before I'd fault you. I know how hard it's been since Joe died. So how about I pick you up in the morning. Say tennish?

ANGELA
I really should think about it more.

BRIAN
This is for Joey's protection as well as yours. Actually he's old enough to have his own hand gun.

ANGELA
My son does not need a gun.

BRIAN
He's in more danger than you are.

ANGELA
I'll get a gun myself. I'll protect him.

Holly and Hank have entered.

HOLLY
What's this about guns?

ANGELA
Excuse me. Nature calls.

She's quickly out of there, to avoid Holly.

HOLLY
Brian? Why are you talking to her about guns?

BRIAN
Because she needs one.

HOLLY
There will be no guns in this house.

BRIAN
Too late.
He reveals a side arm.
I've been packing for almost a year.

HANK
Legal, too, I bet.

BRIAN
Of course it's legal.

HOLLY
I need to sit down a minute. This is happening too fast for me.

She goes to a chair.

BRIAN
I'll come by in the morning to pick up Angela.

He heads out.

HANK
He's doing as well as can be expected.

BRIAN
Pardon me?

HANK
Joey. In case you give a shit about how your nephew is doing. (They stare at one another.)

Blackout.

Scene 10

Darkness.

AUDIO
Twenty-nine percent of world fisheries are in collapse, according to a study by Canadian scientists. The majority could be gone by 2040, they warn. This loss, coupled with a projected doubling of food demand, means farm land animals will have to supply an additional 100 million tons of meat - and this at a time when world farmland also is in crisis. The challenge facing the coming generation of farmers is unprecedented. This is the Guardian Radio Network.

Lights up.
A few days later.
Hank is shooting video of Joey. Joey sits, his crutches nearby.

JOEY
Hi, this is Joey with my first video since coming home from the hospital. I want to thank everybody for the cards and letters and flowers and gifts, More than I can possibly answer. So consider this a big thank you to everybody.

One funny thing. I got a marriage proposal. I didn't know how to respond to that one.

Obviously I'm not going to be marching with you for a while. I don't think I could even if I could walk. My energy has tanked. Most days I just want to sleep or play video games or gin rummy with my uncle. I know I probably should be giving you a pep talk here but sometimes it's hard to keep a lot of thoughts in my head.

Just know, when you're marching and protesting, I'm with you in spirit. That's all for now.

HANK
Cut....Game of gin?

JOEY
I'm going back to bed.

Hank watches as he leaves, walking as best he can with the crutches. Blackout.

Lights up.
A few hours later. Hank and Joey play cards.

JOEY
When did you know you were an artist?

HANK
Actually I never use the word.

JOEY
How come?

HANK
Because the way it's used now has little to do with my understanding of art. An artist is someone who makes art. But art has become a commodity in the marketplace. I find that notion a little obscene.

JOEY
What do you think art is?

HANK
I think J.D. Salinger put it best.

JOEY
Who's he?

HANK
You never read The Catcher in the Rye?

JOEY
No, but I heard of it. It's an important novel, right?

HANK
Well, it once was. Salinger said an artist aims for perfection according to his own standards and no one else's. Art has nothing to do with the marketplace.

JOEY
But you've sold stuff, right?

HANK
I have. But not enough to live on. That's why I teach.

JOEY
But you all are going to be rich. You won't have to teach.

HANK
I'm well aware of this, believe me.

JOEY
How rich is mom going to be?

HANK
Considerably rich.

JOEY
How much is that?

HANK
High six digits.

JOEY
Mom's getting almost a million dollars?

HANK
Don't tell her I told you.

JOEY
Does that mean we have to move to some fancy condo?

HANK
I don't know what her plans are but that doesn't sound like your mother. I'm sure a good chunk of it is going to your college education.

JOEY
Why do people keep making plans when the planet is dying?

Angela and Holly enter.

HOLLY
Hank, you won't believe how high rents are out there. And try buying a house. Who can afford to live here?

JOEY
People who sell their family heritage.

ANGELA
Since when do you care about family roots?

JOEY
I'm just answering the question. Are we going to have to move now?

ANGELA
Of course not.

JOEY
Promise?

ANGELA
We certainly won't move until you graduate.

HANK
Gin. And game. Another?

Joey arranges his crutches and will leave.

JOEY
I need to update my Facebook page.

HANK
How are your members hanging in?

JOEY
Just terrific. Who doesn't like having the crap beat out of them? Who doesn't like their mother being called a whore? It's just awesome to live in the land of the free.

He exits.

ANGELA
That's a perfect example of what I was telling you. His whole attitude is different.

HOLLY
Look what he's been through. I think we're fortunate it's not worse.

ANGELA
Is he this cynical when you're alone with him?

HANK
No.

ANGELA
Does he resent me getting so much money?

HOLLY
How does that make sense?

HANK
I think it's a couple of things. He needs stability in his life now more than ever. That's what this house, his room, provide. Things he can count on. And he must be depressed by the backlash after the march. For the briefest moment at the party, after the march and before the attack, he must have felt like GABI was really going to make a difference. That must have been euphoric. And now ...

HOLLY
I think he made a difference. Congress is finally debating what to do. The kids put that in motion.

HANK
It's a far cry from what he expected.

ANGELA
Then it's time he learned how life can be.

HOLLY
Tell me about it.

HANK
Everybody's under so much pressure today. It's like there's this hunger hovering over the country, an insatiable hunger to have life matter, a hunger for opportunity and a level playing field, and when we don't find what we expect, hunger festers into frustration and lashes out, hunger strikes whatever is in front of it, and you end up with road rage and domestic abuse and random killing ... Under the circumstances, Joey's doing pretty well.

A silence.

                    HOLLY
Anybody want to go out?

                    ANGELA
I'm going to bed early.

                    HANK
I'm game.

                    HOLLY
How about some place we can dance?

                    HANK
Dancing on the Titanic ...

                    HOLLY
Don't get weird on me.

They head out as Angela watches.
Blackout.

Lights up half.
A few hours later.
Joey, a little drunk, is struggling to record a video selfie. He'll have a hard time keeping his balance, using one crutch.

                    JOEY
  Hi, Amanda. This is Joey. I'm sorry I never sent you the video I promised. It took me longer to get home than I thought. I got the texts you sent way back when but I didn't know how to answer them. I can understand why you stopped sending any. Anyway, I've been thinking about you and thought maybe we could reconnect if you have time to reply to this. You're probably the smartest girl I ever met and I'd like to hear what you think about some of the crazy stuff happening now.

Hank and Holly enter. Joey hears them, turns, loses his balance and falls. They rush to him. They smell the booze.

        HOLLY
Are you drunk?

Blackout.

Scene 11

Darkness.

        VOICE IN DARKNESS: TECUMSEH
This is Tecumseh. When it comes your time to die, be not like those whose hearts are filled with fear of death, so that when their time comes they weep and pray for a little more time to live their lives over again in a different way. Sing your death song and die like a hero going home. This is Tecumseh.

Lights up.
The next day.
Angela, Hank, Holly. A sense of concern.
A half full bottle of whiskey on a table.

        HANK
I don't think anyone should use the word intervention.

        HOLLY
That's what it is.

        HANK
Intervention Lite maybe. But to someone as bright and politically aware as Joey, intervention will bring up all the clichés of self-help books, TV shrinks and all the rest.

ANGELA
What's wrong with that?

HOLLY
Exactly.

HANK
He'll tell himself "consider the source" and blow us off. It'll be enough that he knows we love him and are concerned.

HOLLY
(To Angela)
What do you think?

ANGELA
We agreed to put Hank in charge.

HOLLY
Okay then

HANK
Trust me, I know how his brain will react to this.

The home phone rings. Angela answers.

ANGELA
Hello....Actually we're in the middle of something important....I don't have time to explain....Brian, that's great!....Can I get the information and call you back tonight?
Joey enters, a little hung over.
I have to hang up....I will. Talk to you tonight.

She hangs up. Instead of addressing the inquisitive looks from Hank and Holly, she fetches the whiskey bottle.

          ANGELA
Look what I found in the kitchen cabinet. I remember it being almost full.

          JOEY
I'm sorry.

          ANGELA
That's not enough.

          HANK
Sit down. We need to talk to you.

          JOEY
I can't do this now. My morning already sucks.

          HOLLY
Did something happen?

          JOEY
Twice. So I've had enough hassle for one day, okay?

He starts away, back to his room.

          HANK
Sit down, Joey.

          ANGELA
You sit, young man!

          JOEY
Mom ...

          ANGELA
Sit down!

He does. A beat.

        HANK
What two things happened?

        JOEY
Amanda has a boyfriend.

        HANK
Okay. And the other?

        JOEY
The Indians don't want anything to do with GABI any more. With all the backlash, we've become a burden. The goals are the same but it's time for Indians to do it alone.

        HANK
What do you think about that?

        JOEY
Sorry to shock you, but I think they're right.

        HANK
I'm not shocked at all.

        HOLLY
I'm not shocked but I'm surprised.

        ANGELA
Everybody's changing the subject.

        JOEY
I said I was sorry. I did a really stupid thing. I wasn't thinking. If I'd been thinking, I would have replaced what I took with water.

ANGELA
How often has this happened?

JOEY
Just the one time.

She stares him down.

JOEY
One time with the bottle in the cupboard. I usually use the one out here. You use it yourself so often you never notice.

ANGELA
I am so disappointed in you.

JOEY
I'm disappointed in myself. I can't believe I came up with such a stupid idea.

HANK
Hold it right there. GABI got Congress off its ass and today it's facing issues and debating concrete proposals that it should have been dealing with years ago.

ANGELA
Don't flatter him. It was a stupid idea.

HANK
I will never believe that. Don't listen to her.

Joey will struggle to his feet to make a slow exit on his crutches.

JOEY
Since I don't have to listen to her ...

ANGELA
I'm making you an appointment with a professional.

JOEY
Don't be afraid of the word, mom. With a shrink.

ANGELA
Sit down.

JOEY
You think I'm going crazy.

ANGELA
We're not done here.

JOEY
My only problem is I live in a country that keeps lying to itself.

ANGELA
Joseph Stanley Hart!

JOEY
(Reciting)
"Give me your tired, your poor
Your huddled masses yearning to breathe free,
The wretched refuse of your teeming shore.
Send these, their homeless, tempest-toss't to me,
I lift my lamp beside the golden door!"
He starts singing.
"O say can you see, by the dawn's early light ..."
And he's gone.

HOLLY
Somebody tell me that never happened.

A silence.

HANK
What did Brian want?

ANGELA
Excuse me?

HANK
The phone call. You said you'd call him back tonight about something.

ANGELA
Right. The money's almost ready. He needs to know if you want a check or direct deposit.

HANK
Direct deposit.

ANGELA
He'll need the numbers.

HOLLY
Me, too. Straight into the bank.

ANGELA
Somehow a check feels more real than numbers on a computer screen.

A silence.

ANGELA
I thought money was supposed to make you feel better.

Blackout.

Scene 12

Darkness.

VOICE IN DARKNESS: BLACK ELK
This is Black Elk. I did not know then how much was ended. When I look back now from this high hill of my old age, I can still see the butchered women and children lying heapen and scattered all along the crooked gulch as plain as when I saw them with eyes still young. And I can see that something else died there in the bloody mud and was buried in the blizzard. A people's dream died there. It was a beautiful dream. Now the nation's hoop is broken and scattered. There is no center any longer, and the sacred tree is dead. This is Black Elk.

Lights up.
The next day.
Angela and Holly sit.
Hank enters with a grocery sack. He takes out a large bag of candy.

HANK
I got two to be safe.

ANGELA
Did you use the coupon?

HANK
Forget and get the wrath of my sister? No way. Where do you want them?

ANGELA
Just leave them on the kitchen counter.

Hank exits.

HOLLY
You're so prepared. I never remember to get it until the last

minute.

ANGELA
That's why the coupons expire a week before Halloween. They want you to buy early.

Hank returns.

HANK
Obviously he hasn't come out yet.

ANGELA
I heard him in the bathroom.

HANK
And he gave no clue what this is about?

HOLLY
Maybe he wants to apologize. Hopefully.

ANGELA
Here he comes ...

Joey enters on his crutches. He sits down.

JOEY
Thanks for doing this.

ANGELA
What is it we're doing exactly?

JOEY
Helping me get my act together. Sorry about yesterday. I really wigged out. But I have an idea how I can get my life together.

HOLLY
That's encouraging. Right?

HANK
What's the plan?

JOEY
I want to go to college in Sweden.

ANGELA
You can't be serious.

JOEY
Why not? You can afford it now. Can't some of the money be used for what I want?

ANGELA
Most of the money will be used to help you. Not only college but I'm having ramps built so you can get around easier. I'm adding a larger room for you in back and using your present room for guests. Don't you accuse me of being selfish with the money.

A silence.

HANK
What do you want to study in Sweden?

JOEY
I want to become a writer.

HANK
What brought this on?

JOEY
What you told me about art once. How an artist strives for perfection according to his own values. In other words, nobody's telling him how to do his art. Or how to live his life.

HANK
It's a little more complicated than that.

ANGELA
You don't have to go to Sweden to become a writer.

JOEY
I can't live here any more.

HOLLY
Why? We have lots of good writers.

JOEY
It's impossible to live in America without being part of the problem.

HANK
Come on.

JOEY
Look at all of you. You don't even know what you're doing. The clothes you wear - how do you think they're manufactured? How do you think cell phones are assembled? Or coffee beans harvested? You can't do anything without supporting sweatshops that exploit children--

HANK
Hold on, hold on. Listen to yourself. You're too damn smart not to see how much you're exaggerating the problem. Which has been recognized, by the way.

JOEY
Because Nike got caught and claims to have fixed everything? Do you believe them? Do corporations have a history of telling the truth? Do governments have a history of telling the truth?

ANGELA
What is your point?

JOEY
My point is, we're all slaves marching to a corporate drummer. Mr. Franks calls us a new species: Homo consumerus.

HOLLY
Joey, I think you've been brainwashed.

JOEY
By Mr. Franks? At least he makes an effort to understand history. Do any of you do that? How do you deal with your heritage being about stealing America and then trying to exterminate the natives who lived here first? How do you deal with the political coup that killed President Kennedy and overthrew the government?

ANGELA
Kennedy was shot by Oswald.

JOEY
Mom, that's what they want you to believe but it's not what happened. I'm not making this up. There's evidence all over the place. Every doctor that saw the body come into the emergency room said the back of his head had been blown off by a shot from the front. A film shows--

HOLLY
(Interrupting)
Many of us realize there was a conspiracy, Joey.

JOEY
Exactly. But nobody does anything about it. Doesn't history count for anything? Aren't we supposed to learn from it? Corporations poison the air and water and land, they exploit

children, but we still buy the products. The only way to live a moral life in America is to be a Zen monk on a hunger strike.

>   ANGELA
> I try very hard to be careful about what I buy.

>   JOEY
> Mom, you're in the ozone so much you don't even notice when I steal your booze. When's the last time you checked on your hand gun?

>   ANGELA
> What about my gun?

>   JOEY
> I've had it in my room for over a week.

>   ANGELA
> Why?

>   JOEY
> Why do you think?

He begins the process of getting up and leaving on his crutches.

>   ANGELA
> This is the last straw. I'm getting you some help.

>   JOEY
> If you want to help me, send me to Sweden. I'm tired of being part of the problem.

>   ANGELA
> You are not going to Sweden.

>   JOEY
> When I'm eighteen, I can go anywhere I want.

ANGELA
But that's not today.

HANK
Joey, can you and I talk privately?

JOEY
Sorry, my appointment calendar's full ...

He exits.

ANGELA
This is the last straw. I'm calling 911. I'm taking him to the emergency room.

HANK
Let me talk to him first.

ANGELA
All we've done is talk.

HANK
At least let me get the gun back. Angela, I can deal with him.

ANGELA
In five minutes I'm calling 911.

Hank hurries off.

ANGELA
I'm calling now.

HOLLY
Give him five minutes like you said.

ANGELA
Not one second more.

A silence.

HOLLY
You never told me you were redecorating the house.

ANGELA
I made it up as I was talking.

HOLLY
It's a wonderful idea.

The sound of a single GUN SHOT.

ANGELA
Oh my God ...
(Close to collapse)
No, no ...

HOLLY
Angela, it's probably just an accident ...

ANGELA
Dear God, no ...

HOLLY
Hank will make sure everything's okay ...

Hank appears. He's in a state of shock.

HANK
Call 911. Call the police.

Holly will make the call.

ANGELA
Hank?

HANK
... I go in his room, he has the gun to his head ... I say, Joey, put down the gun, you don't want to do this ... I definitely want to do this, he says ... Joey, if you really wanted to do this, you'd have done it by now. Hesitation means you don't ... Uncle Hank, you don't know what it's like, I truly want to ... No, Joey, you don't because it's not that hard, all it takes is pulling the trigger ... So he pulled the trigger ... I think I killed him ...

Blackout.

Scene 13

Darkness.

AUDIO
Futurist Malcolm Peters of MIT calls himself an optimist. Despite the social and political breakdown affecting one third of the Earth's population, despite widespread famine, riots over food and water shortages, Peters sees a bright future. "You can't stifle the human spirit," he says. "You can't stop human ingenuity from getting itself out of the most hopeless looking jams." Peters believes the colonization of Mars will begin in his lifetime. This is the Guardian Radio Network.

Lights up.
Halloween.
Holly shoots video of Angela.

ANGELA
Hello. This is Angela Hart. I'm Joey's mother. I've just come home from the memorial service for my son, and I wanted all his many followers on Facebook to know how perfect it was. So

many people spoke, especially young people, and all of them were so flattering to Joey. He was called a pioneer. He was called a visionary. He was called a saint. One young man, an Indian, from North Dakota, or maybe it was South Dakota, with the most beautiful long silky black hair, which wasn't even braided, and one of those lovely poetic names that Indians sometimes have, something about the sky, he said that Joey was the reddest white man he ever met.

Near the end of his life, Joey told us he wanted to be a writer. I had no idea, but we found a lot of writing in his room. His uncle thought I should read something. He picked out this one.

"The profound silence ... Of a dark night ... Is like solar energy ... For the soul"

Joey had a religious side, a spiritual side, he didn't share with many people. He never shared it with me.
She is close to losing it ... Recovers.

I'm not very Facebook literate, so I don't know what happens to this page with Joey gone, but hopefully some of you can see this message before they take it down.

Please keep the memory of my son alive in your hearts. Thank you.

Holly stops taping.

          HOLLY
Are you okay?

         ANGELA
I'll be fine.

Hank and Brian enter from front door.

         BRIAN
I've been in this racket a long time, and I'm telling you an opportunity like this only comes your way once in a lifetime.

ANGELA
I'm getting into something comfortable before the trick or treaters come.

She exits.

BRIAN
Once in a lifetime, Hank.

HANK
I'll give it serious thought.

BRIAN
So are we going out for dinner or what?

HOLLY
Angela and I are staying home for the trick or treaters.

BRIAN
People still do that? How about breakfast then? My flight doesn't leave until noon.

HANK
Sounds good to me.

BRIAN
I'll give a holler in the morning. Opportunity, brother.

He exits.

HANK
I can't remember the last time he called me brother. He must be desperate.

HOLLY
What opportunity?

                    HANK
He wants me to invest in his new project.

                    HOLLY
Which is?

                    HANK
Some new car technology I don't understand. The air the car pushes through as you drive somehow generates energy and combines with solar to make a car that never needs fuel. Brian says it's a game changer.

                    HOLLY
Wow.

Angela enters. She's been crying.

                    HOLLY
Sis, what's wrong?

                    ANGELA
I'll be alright. I was just thinking about how much fun the kids will have tonight and what a terrible job we've done giving them a decent world to grow up in.

The doorbell rings.

                    HANK
Our first customers.

                    ANGELA
I'll be alright. Holly, would you bring the candy bowl?

The doorbell rings again.
The threesome exit to answer it.
Blackout.

Lights up.
A few hours later. Everybody sitting, waiting.

HANK
I'd say we're done here.

ANGELA
Let me check that no one's down the street.

She exits.

HOLLY
How are you doing? You seem a little better to me.

HANK
I think I am. I'm giving myself a vacation.

HOLLY
Good for you. Where are you going?

HANK
I'm touring the art galleries of Europe next spring.

HOLLY
That's fantastic! I wish I could think of something appropriate like that.

HANK
Finish your degree and get a job teaching theater.

HOLLY
What kind of recommendation are you? All you did was complain about how teaching took too much of your time.

HANK
It's different, you're in a collaborative art form. It would be like having your own subsidized theater company. Access to all

the actors you need, you can direct them, act with them, write for them, all with no demands from the marketplace. Sounds pretty good to me.

        HOLLY
I never thought of it that way.

        HANK
You don't look very excited.

        HOLLY
The world's in such a mess. There's so much suffering. Who am I to have a future?

        HANK
Wrong question. The world is what it is. You can't fix it. The question is, How are you going to spend your time?

        HOLLY
Dance on the Titanic?

        HANK
And try not to step on your partner's toes.

Angela enters.

        HANK
Are we done?

        ANGELA
One more.

Entering behind her is a very old man. He wears the Halloween costume of an Indian chief. He holds a trick or treat bag.

        HALLOWEEN CHIEF
Only after the last tree has been cut down. Only after the last

river has been poisoned. Only after the last fish has been caught. Only then will you learn that money cannot be eaten.

Trick or treat?

Blackout. The play is over.

ABOUT THE PLAYS

Family Values is a major reworking of a much earlier play, which was produced in 1998 under the title *Famililly* and won several competitions. Still, I was not satisfied with it. Now I am.

The Old Beatnik was inspired by my determination to give the Beatniks their due, especially the female poets. As a character says in the play, the hippies were a sell out.

Family Climate is a play I call my six-day wonder, a gift from the gods on my 76th birthday. I woke up on that day with the play whole in my mind. I "transcribed" it in a home bustling with a house guest, conversing as I performed what seemed like secretarial chores. In six days it was done. I got feedback from a number of colleagues and changed little.

I am an old man. I do not expect to write any more plays. These, then, are my last ones. I offer them with a sense of pride and satisfaction.

www.ingramcontent.com/pod-product-compliance
Lightning Source LLC
LaVergne TN
LVHW051045080426
835508LV00019B/1711